Before We Understood

A Memoir

*On Becoming, Faith,
and the Quiet Shape of Love*

MARK IRABOR

Mark Irabor

Scripture taken from the King James Version (KJV). Copyright © 2017
By Thomas Nelson Publishing. Used by permission.

ISBN: 979-8-9897932-4-2 (Paperback)
ISBN: 979-8-9897932-5-9 (Ebook – EPUB)
Library of Congress Control Number: 2026902789

MarkJoy Publishing LLC
P. O. BOX 73741
Houston, TX 77273
For more information, visit markirabor.com

Cover Design: Daniel A. Irabor
Editor: Chelsia McCoy/*Your Writing Table*
Publisher's Cataloging-in-Publication data

Names: Irabor, Mark, author.
Title: Before we understood: a memoir / Mark Irabor.
Series: The Becoming Memoirs
Description: Houston, TX: MarkJoy Publishing, LLC, 2026
Identifiers: LCCN: 20266902789 | ISBN: 979-8-98997932-4-2 (paperback) | 979-8-98997932-5-9 (ebook)
Subjects: LCSH Irabor, Mark. | Irabor, Deborah Joy. | Businesspeople--United States--Biography. | Nigerian Americans--Biography. | African American clergy--Texas--Biography. | Clergy--Biography. | Christian living. | Spiritual biography. | BISAC BIOGRAPHY & AUTOBIOGRAPHY / Memoirs | BIOGRAPHY &

Before We Understood

AUTOBIOGRAPHY / Religious | RELIGION / Christian Living / Inspirational
Classification: LCC BR1725 .I73 2026 | DDC 270.092--dc23

Printed in the United States of America

Dedication

This book is dedicated to those who learned too late what their hearts had tried to teach them early, to those who loved sincerely, waited quietly, and carried unanswered questions longer than they expected. It is for those who wrestled with faith, timing, and identity, and discovered that clarity often arrives only after loss or change has created distance.

These pages honor the silent seasons, the conversations that never happened, and the moments that reshaped us without asking permission. May this work stand as a quiet companion to anyone still becoming, offering grace for what was misunderstood, compassion for what was endured, and hope that meaning, though delayed, is never denied.

Table of Contents

Chapter One 9
Chapter Two 21
Chapter Three 29
Chapter Four 34
Chapter Five 38
Chapter Six 42
Chapter Seven 46
Chapter Eight 51
Chapter Nine 55
Chapter Ten 62
Chapter Eleven 70
Chapter Twelve 77
Chapter Thirteen 81
Chapter Fourteen 85
Chapter Fifteen 90
Chapter Sixteen 96
Chapter Seventeen 101
Chapter Eighteen 107
Chapter Nineteen 113
Chapter Twenty 120
Chapter Twenty-One 128
Chapter Twenty-Two 136
Chapter Twenty-Three 143

Chapter Twenty-Four 149

Chapter Twenty-Five 152

Chapter Twenty-Six 155

Chapter Twenty-Seven 163

Chapter Twenty-Eight 169

Chapter Twenty-Nine 175

Chapter Thirty 182

Chapter Thirty-One 188

Chapter Thirty-Two 194

Chapter Thirty-Three 199

Chapter Thirty-Four 205

Chapter Thirty-Five 211

Chapter Thirty-Six 215

Chapter Thirty-Seven 222

Chapter Thirty-Eight 226

Acknowledgements 233

Coming Soon! 234

CHAPTER ONE
The Journey Before You

"Hey, Mark!"

"Hello, Martin. How are you?" I said, returning the greeting of an old high school science classmate.

"Have you checked the results of the final exams?" Martin asked.

"Not yet," I replied. "I'll check them shortly."

"You passed," he said confidently. "I always knew you would."

He paused, then asked, "So, what are your plans after high school?"

"I plan to attend a university here in Nigeria," I answered. "What about you?"

"I'm going to the Blue Devils," Martin replied excitedly.

"The Blue Devils?" I asked, puzzled. "I don't understand. Explain."

"I'm going to the Blue Devils," he repeated.

"I still don't understand what you mean," I replied, confused.

Without another word, he reached into his bag and pulled out an admission package. The cover featured a basketball mascot of Dillard University's Blue Devils.

"So, you're planning to attend Dillard University in the United States?" I asked.

"Yes," he replied.

Leaving Nigeria to further my education had never crossed my mind. "Well, good luck," I said, turning to walk away.

After I had taken a few steps, I heard him call out, "Mark."

I turned back.

"I have two admission application packages," he said, extending one toward me. "Here, take one. Just in case you need it. You never know."

I accepted the application, nodded, and said, "Thank you. Good luck, and safe travels."

Long before our paths ever crossed, long before I knew the sound of your laughter, the warmth of your voice, or the quiet way your presence would one day anchor my life, my story was already being shaped in ways I could not yet understand.

Looking back now, it feels almost mystical, as though life itself was gently preparing me for you, guiding my steps with unseen hands. But at the time, nothing felt extraordinary. I was simply a young man in Nigeria, searching for direction, uncertain of what the future might hold.

Before We Understood

I didn't wake up one morning expecting my life to change. I felt no clear pull of destiny, no dramatic sign that something significant was unfolding beyond my awareness. I only knew that I stood at the threshold of adulthood, carrying hopes still unformed, trying like so many others, to make sense of my dreams and the life ahead.

Since I can remember, I wanted to be a doctor. The desire didn't come from movies or prestige; it came from witnessing suffering, from seeing people I loved depend on under-resourced clinics, from a sense deep inside me that healing was a calling rather than a profession. To me, medicine represented purpose. It meant stepping into the chaos of life and offering calm. It meant learning the delicate skill of holding another person's pain.

Naturally, my plans revolved around studying in Nigeria, attending one of the respected medical schools, and building my life from there. I researched universities thoroughly, reading their programs and imagining myself sitting in their classrooms, wearing the white coat I had dreamed of since childhood. I applied confidently, believing the next steps would fall into place.

But nothing prepared me for the unexpected source of resistance: my father. He had his own vision of where I should go, shaped by tradition, experience, and the values he held. In his eyes, certain universities represented prestige, structure, and a clear path. But those were not the schools I felt drawn to.

What followed were days of debate, weeks of discussion, and months of tension. My father dismissed the universities I had chosen, insisting I attend the local university where I lived. I stood firm, trying to explain why the schools appealed to me and how I connected with their mission, but it didn't matter. His answers were firm, final, and difficult to challenge.

The conflict surprised me. My father and I had disagreed before, but never about anything that would shape the foundation of my future. At first, I believed time would soften his position. But instead, the disagreement grew larger, filling our home with unspoken frustration.

Late at night, I rehearsed arguments in my mind, imagining the conversation going differently, imagining him understanding what the decision meant to me. But every attempt ended the same way.

Days turned into weeks, and weeks slipped into months. While my friends celebrated acceptance letters and made plans for dorm life, I remained suspended in uncertainty. I felt stuck, powerless, and increasingly doubtful about what my future held. My dream, once bright and vivid, began to dim at the edges.

It was during one of those heavy, hushed evenings that a tiny spark of possibility stirred in my mind. At first, it felt fragile, almost too distant to grasp a thought that seemed both foreign and tantalizing. Somewhere on the top shelf of my bedroom closet, buried beneath a messy stack of papers, lay an old application packet for Dillard University in New Orleans, given to me long ago by a high school classmate.

Somehow, that forgotten bundle now seemed charged with a quiet promise, as if waiting for me to notice it. *What if my path isn't here? What if I'm meant to look beyond Nigeria?*

The thought unsettled me. Leaving home had never been part of the plan. Everything I knew, family, food, language, and community, lived in Nigeria. The idea of starting over in another country felt like rewriting my entire existence. But the more the conflict lingered, the more the thought pressed itself against the edges of my mind.

At first, I tried to brush it aside. Studying abroad? In the United States? It sounded grand, ambitious, maybe even unreasonable. But sometimes an idea, once planted, refuses to leave. And this one grew roots quickly.

I found myself researching American universities late into the night, reading about international students who had taken similar leaps of faith. I went to the state ministry of education, where I looked up foreign students' admission requirements, scholarship opportunities, and visa processes, each piece of information pulling me deeper into a world I had never imagined for myself.

When I finally mustered the courage to share my plan with my father, the room seemed to shrink around us. I held my breath, expecting a lecture, a sharp "no," or silence heavy with disappointment. Instead, he was quiet for a long moment, long enough that my heart raced and doubt crept in, whispering that perhaps I had misjudged him. Then, almost casually, he said words that would stay with me forever: "If you want to go, go... but know that you are on your own."

His disapproval wasn't wrapped in anger, nor softened with persuasion. It was simple, measured, and almost indifferent, but that simplicity made it sting all the more. In his own way, he had drawn a line. It felt as though a door I hadn't even realized existed had quietly slammed shut. Everything I had imagined about his support evaporated in that instant, leaving me standing on my own. And yet, despite the fear, a spark of determination flared inside me.

I pressed forward, applying to Dillard University in New Orleans and Texas Southern University in Houston. My heart leaned toward Texas Southern; a close friend had moved there the year before, and the thought of being near someone familiar gave me a sense of comfort amid the uncertainty. I imagined myself walking through its halls, attending classes, and building a life far from the streets of home. I prayed, I hoped, and pictured the acceptance letter in my hands, feeling it as though it had already arrived.

But again, days turned into weeks and the letter from Texas Southern never came. Each day, disappointment settled more heavily in my chest. I found myself pacing my room, staring at the ceiling, replaying conversations with my father, questioning every choice I had made. Was I foolish to hope for a future so far from what I knew? Was this independence worth the loneliness it demanded? Nights were the hardest. In the quiet, I wrestled with fear, with longing, and with a nagging sense that perhaps I had overestimated my courage. Yet even in that solitude, I refused to surrender my dream.

Then, one afternoon, a package arrived. The envelope was unassuming, yet I recognized the logo immediately. My hands trembled as I opened it, and there it was: the acceptance letter from Dillard University. I stared at it for what felt like an eternity, not in disbelief, but in gratitude. Every anxious night, every self-doubt, every moment of uncertainty suddenly made sense. After months of waiting, the first door had opened.

Before We Understood

Holding that letter, I realized something important: the path ahead would not be easy. I would be on my own, just as my father had warned. But for the first time in months, I felt the exhilarating clarity of possibility. I could shape my own future, take my own steps, and meet the challenges ahead with a determination born of knowing I had fought to arrive here.

In that quiet moment, I made a promise to myself. I would not let fear dictate my path. I would not look back. And though the road was still uncertain, the light of that single acceptance letter illuminated a way forward, one I was finally ready to walk.

Besides, I thought the journey was only about education. I did not imagine that this new beginning held something far more profound than academic growth. I had no idea that I was moving toward a love story written before I understood what love truly meant.

A year earlier, long before I understood how profoundly my life was about to change, one of my cousins introduced me to a friend who would later become my own. As he prepared to travel to the United States for school, I found myself walking beside him, observing his steps, listening to his plans, and quietly absorbing the possibility of a future I had not yet imagined for myself. It was not ambition that guided me then, but proximity, simply being close enough to someone whose path was already unfolding.

One day, he suggested that I accompany him to his brother's office to collect money for his passport application. Almost as an afterthought, he encouraged me to apply for a passport as well—just in case I ever decided to travel abroad. At the time, the idea felt distant, almost irrelevant. I had no intention of leaving Nigeria, and more importantly, I had no money to cover the passport application fee or even the cost of the required photographs. Traveling abroad belonged to other people's lives, not mine.

When we arrived at his brother's office, he introduced me and mentioned, almost casually, that I also needed funds for a passport application. What happened next stayed with me. Without hesitation or questioning, his brother provided money not only for the application fee but also for passport photographs, transportation, and even lunch. In that moment, I did not fully grasp the significance of his generosity. Looking back, I see it as one of the quiet interventions that would later define my journey as an unremarkable act on the surface, yet pivotal in its consequence.

With that unexpected support, I began assembling the documents required for a visa interview, moving forward step by step, even though I still did not fully understand where the path might lead. The process itself was exhausting and emotionally demanding. The day before my interview, I travelled for seven long hours by bus from Benin City to Lagos. By the time I arrived at my uncle's house that night, my body was tired, but my mind refused to rest.

My interview was scheduled for 9:30 a.m., but I arrived at the embassy by 6:30 a.m., determined not to risk being late. The hours stretched endlessly as applicant after applicant was called ahead of me. The interview process ran behind schedule, and by the time my name was finally called, the afternoon sun had begun its slow descent. The interview itself was brief, almost anticlimactic. I answered a few questions, handed over my documents, and was told to return to the waiting area.

As I waited, I watched every person who had been interviewed before me walk away with disappointment etched on their faces. One by one, visas were denied. Yet strangely, I did not panic. Instead, a calm settled over me, one that did not come from certainty but from surrender. I felt deeply that God was present in that room, guiding the outcome in ways beyond my control. I told myself that if it was His will, I would receive the visa, and if it was not, I would accept that as well. Either way, I believed I would be okay.

About an hour later, my name was called again. I approached the interview window with measured steps, unsure of what awaited me. When the officer returned my passport with a four-year student visa stamped inside, time seemed to pause. I thanked him, stepped away, and only then allowed myself to breathe. The weight I had been carrying quietly lifted.

The journey back to Benin City was long, but joy made the hours pass more gently. When I arrived home late that night, my parents were seated on the front porch, as they often were. I greeted them and walked toward my room, still holding the news close to my chest. Before I could say anything, I heard my mother's footsteps behind me. She needed to know. When I told her that I had been granted a student visa, her excitement filled the space between us. In that moment, I understood that the journey was no longer mine alone; it belonged to all of us.

Booking the ticket was surreal. Packing my bags felt like closing one chapter and preparing to walk into another. My mother folded clothes with me, her fingers lingering over fabrics as if sealing blessings into them. My siblings asked questions, half-teasing, half-proud. My father stood quietly, watching, his expression unreadable, but his presence alone felt supportive.

On the day of my departure, Nigeria felt both familiar and suddenly foreign, like a place I was not leaving behind forever but stepping away from temporarily. As I climbed the steps of the airplane, my hands trembled not from fear, but from the weight of possibility.

When the plane lifted off the ground, I felt something lift in me as well. I looked out of the window, watching Lagos fade into a motley of lights before disappearing into clouds. I knew I was leaving behind the boy I had been. I didn't yet know the man I was becoming.

The journey felt endless, each hour stretching longer than the last. My first pause came in Amsterdam, Netherlands, where I had a 12-hour stopover. The city's canals glimmered under the soft light, bicycles whizzed past, and the aroma of fresh pastries hinted at life beyond the airport walls. Though brief, the glimpse of the city was a welcome respite from the confines of travel.

The following day, I took to the skies again, my heart heavy yet eager. Ten hours later, after countless clouds and distant sunsets, the vast expanse of the United States unfolded beneath me. Stepping off the plane, a mix of fatigue and excitement washed over me. I had finally arrived.

America greeted me with cold air and unfamiliar accents. The streets were wider, the pace faster, the faces different. Everything felt strange, not bad, just different. I found myself learning new systems: how to take the bus, how to convert Naira to Dollars in my head, how to understand professors who spoke faster than anyone I had ever met. There were days I felt excited, and days I felt invisible. Some nights I lie awake missing home, the food, the rhythms, the comfort of familiar voices.

But I kept going. I built routines. I found small pockets of comfort. I adapted. I grew. And through it all, I had no idea that life was guiding me toward a moment that would change everything, the moment our paths would cross.

Destiny rarely announces itself. It doesn't send signals or warnings. It moves quietly, arranging the pieces of our lives with a patience we don't appreciate until later. While I was navigating a new country, pushing through challenges, and finding my footing, you were living your own story, shaped by your journeys, your victories, your heartbreaks, and your unanswered prayers.

We were both walking down separate roads, unaware that they were curving toward each other. Every choice we made, every delay, every disappointment, every accomplishment pushed us closer to the moment when our stories would merge into one.

There were times when I questioned whether I belonged in the U.S., especially when the loneliness felt heavy. Times when I wondered whether all the challenges were signs that I had made a mistake. But fate is patient. It knew what I did not: that every hardship was simply a stepping stone, shaping me into the version of myself who would one day be ready for you.

Even on the days I felt lost, I was moving toward

something meaningful. Even when nothing made sense, something was quietly unfolding. Even when I doubted myself, Destiny did not doubt its timing.

And then, without warning and without ceremony, everything shifted.

It happened on an ordinary day, a day that started like all the others. I didn't even know that I was walking into a moment that would divide my life into *before* and *after*. I didn't know that the person who would become my peace, my partner, my unexpected blessing, was about to enter my world.

But Destiny knew.

I was simply living my life, unaware that yours was about to collide with mine. Unaware that the journey that began with uncertainty, frustration, and a leap of faith was guiding me straight into the beginning of *our* story. Unaware that the next chapter of my life, our love story, was about to begin.

And in that quiet, unsuspecting moment, everything would change.

CHAPTER TWO
Written Before We Met

While I was still in Nigeria, living day to day with the quiet weight of uncertainty pressing on my thoughts, I often found myself standing at the crossroads of possibility and frustration. I was a young man with a big dream, the dream of becoming a medical doctor, and an even bigger determination to make something meaningful of my life. But determination alone did not clear a path forward. Each step I took felt like walking through tall, thorny grass: slow, painful, and resistant.

I had applied to several universities across Nigeria, pouring effort and patience into each application. I believed that education would open the door to my future, yet every door I hoped to walk through felt shut before I could even reach the handle. My father had strong opinions about the schools I chose. He rejected some outright, discouraged others, and felt none fully aligned with what he wanted for me. His intentions may have been rooted in care and concern, but for me, it created a fog of confusion. I wanted so desperately to move forward, yet I felt held in place, unsure which direction would finally lead somewhere new.

Even in the moments when frustration nearly overwhelmed me, something within whispered that the story was larger than the struggle I could see. Still, I never imagined just how much larger. I never imagined that thousands of miles away, God was arranging the details of a plan that involved not just my future and my education, but my heart and the course of my entire life.

At the same time, while I paced the floors in Nigeria, thinking about university prospects, Deborah was in Northern California, walking her own path, unaware that her decisions would eventually intertwine with mine. She lived in a completely different world, one with its own rhythm and landscape, yet just like me, she was searching for direction.

Deborah had reached a season where she knew it was time to take the next step toward her academic future. She was diligent, focused, and intentional in pursuing her goals. Anyone observing her would have seen a young woman who understood that preparation was as necessary as ambition. She gathered information, consulted her cousin Ernest in New Orleans, spoke with guidance counselors, and prayed for clarity as she considered different colleges.

This was not a simple process for her. She was not just looking for a school; she was looking for the right environment, a place where she could grow academically, emotionally, and spiritually. Over time, her list of potential universities took shape: Bethune-Cookman College in Daytona Beach, Florida; Hampton Institute in Virginia; Loyola University; Tulane University; and Dillard University in New Orleans, Louisiana. Each institution held a unique attraction, a different opportunity, and a slightly different version of who she might become.

Deborah carefully prepared each application request, typing on her old Corona typewriter, writing statements, and organizing paperwork. She dropped them in the mail one by one, a mix of hope and nervous expectation that every young person feels when imagining the next chapter of their life. She knew her future might depend on the response of strangers sitting behind desks far away, and she submitted each request with a silent prayer that God would open the right door.

Among all the universities she considered, Bethune-Cookman College was her favorite, the school that lived in her imagination. She admired its history, legacy, and the vibrant student life she had read about in Ebony Magazine.

The idea of studying in Daytona Beach, surrounded by sunshine and a community that felt warm and welcoming, appealed to her deeply. She envisioned herself walking across the campus courtyard, attending chapel services, forming friendships, and beginning the adult life she had dreamed of.

Still life has a way of redirecting us without warning. As she waited for responses, a mix of anticipation and anxiety settled over her. Days turned into weeks, and weeks slowly stretched into months. Each time she opened the mailbox, she hoped to see an envelope from Bethune-Cookman with the application she wanted. She waited. She prayed. But nothing came from the school she longed for the most.

Of all the applications for admission she had written, she received only three: Loyola, Tulane, and Dillard Universities. Deborah once again typed out two letters of request to both Hampton and Bethune-Cookman, hoping the applications had been lost in the mail. She tried calling the admissions offices at both schools; she was promised the prized application. However, they never arrived before the December 1st admission deadline. Unfortunately, they never came at all.

Instead, one day an envelope arrived from Dillard University, an institution she respected, but had not placed at the very top of her list. She opened the letter expecting another standard response, perhaps an acceptance, perhaps a rejection, or perhaps a notice requesting additional documents. But what she found inside changed the course of her life. Dillard was offering her a Presidential Scholarship.

A full scholarship is not something many people brush aside lightly. It is a blessing, an open door, an unmistakable confirmation that someone believes in your potential. For Deborah, the offer made her pause and think deeply. She had hoped for Bethune-Cookman, prayed for it even, but here was Dillard extending not just acceptance but financial support, a gift that would relieve her and her family of a significant burden.

Still, she waited a little longer. She wanted to give Bethune-Cookman every possible chance to send the application. She continued checking the mailbox with quiet patience, but the silence from Daytona Beach grew louder with each passing day. Eventually, she realized that the time had come to make a choice. And while Bethune-Cookman felt like the school she wanted, Dillard began to feel like the school she was meant to attend.

So, she accepted the scholarship.

At the time, it seemed like a straightforward decision, a practical choice made in the interest of her education and finances. She didn't know that this single acceptance would shape the rest of her life. She didn't know that it would carry her across the country, into classrooms and dormitories she had never seen before, into a community and culture that would transform her. And she certainly did not know that it would guide her into my world, even though that world was thousands of miles away.

Meanwhile, I remained in Nigeria, unaware of the puzzle pieces slowly coming together across the ocean. I was still trying to make sense of my circumstances, still trying to push through obstacles that made no sense to me at the time. But now, looking back, I realize that even when I felt stuck, God was actively moving. Even when I felt I was waiting for something that would never come, events elsewhere were unfolding that would eventually make the waiting worthwhile.

It's remarkable how life works. Two young people living on opposite sides of the world, one facing stalled admission in Africa, the other weighing scholarship choices in America, both taking steps that seemed unrelated, yet both moving closer to the moment when their lives would intersect.

Deborah's acceptance to Dillard University placed her right where she needed to be for our paths to eventually cross. And though neither of us knew it, both of us were being guided by a plan far greater than anything we could have orchestrated alone.

Deborah prepared for her move to New Orleans with a mixture of excitement and nervousness. The idea of attending a historically Black university with such a rich legacy stirred something deep and inspiring within her. She imagined the culture, the music, the food, the traditions, and the academic rigor. But mostly, she wondered what type of person she would become in that environment.

Sometimes we make decisions thinking we are simply choosing a school, a job, or a place to live, not realizing we are choosing the future version of ourselves. Deborah was choosing a chapter she could not yet fully see. She was stepping into the unknown, trusting that the path ahead would shape her into the woman she hoped to become.

As she prepared to leave California, her friends and family celebrated her scholarship, congratulating her on what felt like the beginning of something extraordinary. They help pack her suitcases, offer advice for college life, and remind her to stay focused and grounded. She embraced their encouragement, but a quiet longing remained inside her, an unanswered question about Bethune-Cookman. Why hadn't they responded? Why hadn't the dream she hoped for unfolded?

What she didn't realize was that the silence from Bethune-Cookman was not a denial of her dreams but a redirection toward something, someone, far better than she could have anticipated.

And on the other side of the world, I too was being pushed into a place of redirection. The more I struggled to find a way forward in Nigeria, the more the idea of studying in the United States took root in my mind. It wasn't an easy thought to entertain. Leaving Nigeria meant leaving everything familiar: my family, my friends, my culture, my sense of belonging. But it also meant possibility. It meant a chance to pursue a future that seemed unreachable from where I stood.

Neither Deborah nor I knew that the answers we were seeking, answers about education, purpose, and direction, were intertwined in a way that only time would reveal. The choices we made separately, the frustrations we felt individually, and the prayers we whispered quietly into the night were all converging toward a single destiny that neither of us could have predicted.

Looking back now, it's difficult not to marvel at how every delay, every disappointment, every unanswered letter, and every unexpected opportunity became part of a larger plan. I was in Nigeria feeling stranded. Deborah was in California making choices that would take her to Dillard. We were worlds apart, yet God was guiding both our footsteps with precision, arranging moments and decisions that would eventually bring us to the same place, at the same time, for a purpose neither of us yet understood.

Her acceptance to Dillard University, the only school that offered her a full scholarship, was not simply an academic decision. It was a divine alignment. It was the beginning of a story that had started long before we ever laid eyes on each other. A story that was unfolding silently, beautifully, and intentionally across oceans.

At the time, neither of us knew that our lives had begun to move toward each other. But in hindsight, it is clear:

while I was in Nigeria wrestling with thoughts about my future, and while Deborah was in Northern California preparing for college, God was already writing the first unseen chapters of our love story.

CHAPTER THREE
The Quiet Pull of Destiny

If someone had told me then that my life was already on a collision course with Deborah's, I would have dismissed it as fantasy. At the time, nothing in my daily reality hinted at the profound shift that was coming. I was still in Nigeria, still waking up each morning to the same heat, the same routines, the same anxieties about my future. I still walked the familiar streets of my neighborhood and sat in the same living room listening to the same conversations that left me more frustrated than encouraged.

But beneath the surface of my frustration, something was changing. A subtle restlessness had taken hold of me, one that I could not explain. It wasn't fear or impatience. It was more like a gentle tug on my spirit, as if some unseen force was saying, *"Your future is not here. Not in this place.*

Not in this way."

Every time I thought about staying in Nigeria and continuing to push through roadblocks, my heart grew heavier. But whenever I imagined studying in the United States, a feeling of possibility stirred within me. It was not confidence I did not yet know how I would make such a drastic move happen. But there was a spark of hope, a sense that at least somewhere beyond where I stood, the door to my future was unlocked.

Meanwhile, in Northern California, Deborah entered a season of preparation. Once she accepted Dillard University's scholarship, everything around her seemed to accelerate. The spring became a series of transitions, packing, planning, and emotional goodbyes.

As she prepared to leave home, she began to understand something that only becomes clear when you take a significant step away from everything you've known: that growth often begins the moment you step into the unknown.

Her family supported her fully. Her mother told her she was proud. Her friends threw her a small farewell gathering and their laughter was loud enough to mask the bittersweet undertone that lingered in the background. They hugged her tightly and promised to stay in touch. She smiled, grateful for their love, but quietly aware that college, especially college across the country, has the power to create distance that few friendships survive.

Still, she was determined. She believed Dillard would shape her, challenge her, and prepare her for the life she envisioned. What she couldn't know then was that the school she had accepted out of practicality would become the setting of her destiny.

As Deborah boarded her flight and watched California disappear beneath the clouds, she had no idea how profoundly New Orleans would impact her life. She had no idea that someone who had not yet left Nigeria was already on a path that would lead directly into hers. She certainly had no idea that the decisions she made in those moments would one day become part of a story much larger and more beautiful than anything she could have imagined at the time.

Across the ocean, my own journey was shifting in quiet ways. The idea of studying in the United States was no longer just a wish; it was becoming a conviction. The thought refused to leave me alone. It followed me into conversations, into my prayers, and into the quiet moments at night when the house settled into silence, and all I could hear was the sound of my own heartbeat.

I started asking questions, one at a time, about how students left Nigeria to study abroad. I listened carefully whenever I heard stories about people who had gone to school in America. The idea still seemed impossible, but it no longer felt unreachable. It felt like a mountain I had not yet figured out how to climb, yet one meant for me to attempt.

My father remained unaware of these internal shifts. He still believed my future lay in Nigerian universities, the ones he approved of, the ones he felt comfortable with. But I felt something stirring in me that I could not quiet. God was nudging me, even if I did not yet fully recognize it. He was gently loosening the soil beneath my feet, preparing me for the journey ahead.

Immediately after graduation, Deborah arrived in New Orleans. She stepped into a world that pulsed with culture and history. The humid air wrapped around her like a warm embrace. She heard students laughing, cars honking, and the distant echoes of music drifting from somewhere off-campus. Dillard University, with its stately buildings and rich legacy, felt alive in a way that made her heart beat just a little faster.

After a summer spent visiting relatives in both New Orleans and Mississippi, Deborah had the opportunity to acclimate herself to her new southern surroundings.

Orientation week was a swirl of introductions, forms to sign, campus tours, and new faces. Deborah tried to take it all in while walking across the shaded pathways lined with centuries-old oak trees. She felt the deep sense of community on campus, the spiritual undertones, the pride, the resilience woven into the school's identity.

Every student she encountered stood at the edge of a new beginning, unaware that their paths were already being shaped by forces beyond their understanding. She did not yet know that her own journey would one day intersect with that of a young man from another continent, and that their meeting had been written long before either of them arrived.

I reached a point where I realized I could no longer ignore the quiet pull on my heart. I needed to look beyond the boundaries of my comfort, beyond the expectations of those around me. I needed to take a leap. But what I did know was that my future was not confined to the walls closing in around me. Something inside me kept whispering that the life I craved, the purpose I felt drawn to, was waiting elsewhere. I didn't see the whole picture, not even a fraction of it. I only felt the call.

Before We Understood

Little did I know that call was leading me on a path toward Deborah, toward a woman I had never met, whose name I didn't know, whose face I had never seen, but who was already becoming part of my story long before she ever entered my life.

Destiny is often silent, but it is never still.

And in those quiet moments, Deborah began her journey at Dillard, and I contemplated a path to the United States; our futures, still unseen, were slowly aligning.

CHAPTER FOUR
The Moment We Met

It was a quiet evening at Dillard University in New Orleans. The campus had settled into that calm lull that comes after classes end and students retreat to their dorms. The cafeteria was not crowded, just a few scattered groups, the hum of low conversation blending with the clatter of trays and silverware. I had just finished waiting in line, picking up my food, and was searching for a spot to eat in peace, lost in my thoughts and anticipation about classes, homework, and the challenges of adapting to life in a new country.

I found an empty table in a corner, away from the bustle, and quietly sat down. I remember feeling the subtle weight of loneliness that sometimes-accompanied studying abroad, that strange mixture of excitement and isolation. I had been so focused on my studies, on adapting to a new culture, that I had not really allowed myself to notice just how much I longed for connection, someone who could break through the walls I had built around myself.

And then she appeared.

She was walking toward me, her presence somehow luminous in the soft cafeteria light. I noticed her first by the way she carried herself, confident yet approachable, with a calm grace that immediately drew attention without seeking it. She stopped at the edge of my table, a small, polite smile on her face.

"Is it okay if I sit here?" she asked, her voice gentle, friendly.

I looked up, startled for a moment; this was unusual. I hadn't expected company. But there was something in her eyes that made the decision easy. I nodded. "Sure," I said, a small smile tugging at my lips.

She slid into the seat across from me, placing her tray carefully in front of her. "I'm Deborah Joy Ford," she said, extending her hand.

I shook it warmly, trying to hide the surprise I felt at the sudden connection. "I'm Mark Irabor," I replied.

There was a brief pause, the kind that feels comfortable rather than awkward, as though the world had momentarily slowed down just for us. Then, with genuine curiosity, she asked, "Where are you from?"

"Nigeria," I said, and I noticed her eyes light up at the word.

She leaned forward slightly. "Oh, that's amazing! How do you say hello in your language?"

I smiled, pleased by her interest. "You say 'Hello'... or in Nigerian slang, we might say '*Wishone.*"

"*Wishone?*" she repeated, attempting the pronunciation with a careful, sweet tone. Her laughter, soft and musical, broke the quiet atmosphere in the cafeteria, and I couldn't help but laugh along with her.

And just like that, we began to talk.

What started as small talk quickly blossomed into a conversation that felt effortless, as if we had known each other far longer than just a few minutes. We exchanged stories about our families, our backgrounds, and the paths that had brought us to Dillard University. She spoke of her childhood in California, her dreams, and the experiences that had shaped her. I shared glimpses of my life in Nigeria, my family, my studies, my journey to the United States, and my struggles and triumphs along the way.

The cafeteria around us seemed to fade into the background. I was no longer aware of the distant chatter, the clinking trays, or the fluorescent lights above. Everything shrank until it was just the two of us, talking, laughing, and discovering each other.

At one point, she asked me about my favorite Nigerian foods. I described jollof rice, pounded yams, and Egusi soup, painting pictures with words as best I could. She listened intently, asking questions and teasing me gently when I struggled to explain certain flavors or cultural nuances.

"I have to try it someday," she said, smiling. "You'll have to teach me how to say more words in your native language, too."

"I'd be happy to," I replied. "But be careful, you might start speaking more Nigerian than American English."

Her laughter was easy and unrestrained. It was the kind of sound that made a room feel warmer, brighter, alive. And in that moment, I realized something extraordinary: I wanted to hear that laugh again, to continue this conversation far longer than the evening would allow.

As we talked, I noticed subtle details about her, the way her eyes sparkled with curiosity, the thoughtful tilt of her head when she listened, the genuine way she engaged with my words. It was rare to meet someone whose presence felt both comforting and invigorating. For the first time in a long while, I felt seen entirely.

When the evening drew on, and the cafeteria began to empty, neither of us wanted the conversation to end. We exchanged dorm information, promising to meet again, to continue what had started as a simple conversation over dinner trays. Walking back to my dorm later that night, I couldn't stop replaying the encounter in my mind, each word and laugh echoing in a way that felt almost magical. Looking back now, that evening in the cafeteria feels like a moment suspended in time. It was ordinary in setting, just two students sharing a table, but extraordinary in impact.

I had come to Dillard University seeking an education, a degree, a future built on knowledge and opportunity.

What I hadn't anticipated was that I would find someone who would alter the course of my life in ways I couldn't have imagined.

It was the quiet evening, the unassuming cafeteria, the simple question, "Is it okay if I sit here?" and the answer that started everything: "Sure."

And so began our story, a story that had been unfolding long before we met, now stepping into the light in the most unexpected, wonderful way.

CHAPTER FIVE
Crossing Paths Again

In the weeks that followed, our paths continued to align in ways that seemed almost magical. History classes became a space for lively debates. She had a sharp mind and wasn't afraid to challenge others' perspectives, which I secretly admired. Our discussions often ended in laughter. Algebra, on the other hand, presented its own challenges to Deborah, but it was one of my favorite subjects. We would sit together after class, working through problems, exchanging tips, and occasionally teasing each other as we worked on solving an equation.

Her words, light as they were, carried an understated intensity that I couldn't ignore. I realized that these small moments, playful exchanges, and shared frustrations were becoming the highlights of my days. I was looking forward to every class, every lab, every interaction. It was no longer just about the studies; it was about being near her, about learning alongside her, about experiencing life in a way that felt richer because she was there.

Our friendship grew naturally, effortlessly, yet there was an undercurrent I couldn't name. I found myself lingering on her words, replaying conversations in my mind, imagining scenarios in which our connection deepened. Sometimes I caught myself staring a little too long when she laughed, or feeling a rush of warmth when she looked my way. Every shared joke, every thoughtful comment, every glance carried a weight I was only beginning to understand.

Even casual walks across campus became opportunities for connection. We would discuss lectures, share favorite authors, talk about music, and exchange stories of childhood experiences. I learned about her family, her passions, and the small moments that had shaped her. She, in turn, listened to my stories of Nigeria, my family, my culture, my struggles, and the journey that had brought me to Dillard University. Each conversation strengthened a bond that felt both inevitable and fragile, as though we were walking a tightrope between friendship and something far more profound.

One evening, after a long day of classes, we sat together on a bench outside the library, the cool breeze of New Orleans brushing against our faces. The campus rested in silence as the sun dipped low, leaving behind a soft, golden light.

"You know," she said thoughtfully, "I'm really glad we

ended up in the same classes."

"Me too," I replied, my voice low. "It feels... right, somehow. Like we were meant to cross paths more than once."

She smiled, a little shyly, and looked away toward the trees lining the walkway. "It does feel that way. I didn't expect to meet someone like you here."

Her words lingered, filling the space between us with an unspoken acknowledgment. I wanted to say more, to tell her that I had been thinking about her since the cafeteria, that each encounter since then had pulled me closer, but I hesitated. There was a delicate balance between the comfort of friendship and the risk of revealing too much too soon.

Besides, the pull between us was undeniable. Every day, every class, every shared laugh added to the momentum, building an invisible bridge between our lives. Even in silence, we communicated in glances, smiles, and the small gestures that only two people growing close could share.

What had begun as chance encounters had blossomed into a bond that neither of us could ignore. We were no longer simply classmates sharing assignments; we had become companions in the truest sense. We laughed together, struggled together, and navigated the complexities of college life side by side. And through it all, there was a quiet anticipation—a sense that the story unfolding between us was only beginning, and that something deeper, something extraordinary, awaited just beyond the horizon.

Looking back now, it is clear that the universe had been

orchestrating these moments long before we realized it. The cafeteria meeting, the shared classes, the labs, the study sessions, all of it was more than a coincidence. It was the careful threading of fate, slowly drawing two people together and laying the foundation for a story neither of us could have imagined.

And in those moments, laughing over lab mistakes, debating history, working through algebra, and sharing quiet conversations on campus benches, I felt it: the undeniable sense that life was leading me to something far greater than I had planned. Something that had begun long before I met her and was now quietly, irrevocably taking shape.

CHAPTER SIX
Unexpected Turn

Life at Dillard University moved forward for me in its usual rhythm: classes, assignments, campus events, and long evenings at the library. But she lingered in my mind. It was impossible not to think of her, the way her eyes lit up with curiosity, the musical warmth of her laugh, and the effortless way she engaged with me in those few minutes. That fleeting encounter had planted a seed that began to grow silently in the background of my daily life.

I immersed myself in my studies, keeping busy as I adapted to this new country. Each day presented challenges, adjusting to the fast-paced lectures, navigating unfamiliar cultural norms, and keeping up with demanding coursework, but I couldn't stop thinking about Deborah. Every time I passed a cafeteria table or heard a soft, melodic laugh, I wondered: Was it too soon to hope I would see her again?

One day after Biology class, Deborah and I met up and began our usual banter about assignments, teachers, and campus life. We stopped near a quiet bench in front of the library, the golden light of the sun filtering through the leaves. Deborah leaned against the backrest, her eyes searching mine.

"Mark," she said softly, "can I tell you something?"

"Of course," I said, my voice steady, though my chest felt heavy with anticipation.

She hesitated for a moment, her fingers fidgeting with the edge of her notebook. Her eyes met mine, revealing a vulnerability that made my heart tighten. Then, slowly, carefully, she spoke: "I... I am seeing someone right now. I have a boyfriend."

The words landed softly, yet they struck me like a sudden jolt. I blinked, caught between the impulse to speak and the need to process what I had just heard. For a moment, the world seemed to blur around the edges, the glow of the sun outside the library window dimming in my vision.

I forced a small smile, trying to mask the sting I felt. "Oh... okay," I said quietly, my voice steady but my mind racing. Deborah's gaze dropped to her hands, and I could see the tension in her posture, the subtle nervousness in the way she shifted. "I... I didn't want to hide it from you.

I nodded, trying to keep my emotions in check. "I appreciate your honesty," I said. "Really, I do." But inside, my thoughts were a storm. I had felt the pull between us for weeks, the sparks that hinted at something more profound. And now, the very thing I had hoped for—the possibility of something more—was complicated by the reality of her situation.

For a moment, silence hung between us, heavier than words could carry. I searched her face, wanting to see if there was any hint that her feelings might align with mine despite the circumstances. Her eyes flickered, uncertain and apologetic, and I realized that this wasn't a confession meant to hurt me; it was a confession of honesty and trust.

"Deborah," I said finally, choosing my words carefully, "I want you to be happy. That's all I want. And I don't want this to make things awkward between us."

She looked up, relief washing over her features. "Thank you, Mark. That means a lot. I...I really do. But I'm trying to figure things out with him, and I don't want to complicate either of our lives.

The honesty in her voice was almost more painful than the words themselves. I nodded again, swallowing the mix of emotions swirling inside me. "I understand," I said."

Her lips curved into a small, grateful smile, and I felt a pang of longing. We had crossed the boundary between friendship and something more, and yet fate had placed a barrier between us. But I also knew that this wasn't the end of our story; it was a pause, a moment of tension that would only deepen the connection between us over time.

As we left the library later that evening, walking side by side through the campus, I felt the weight of unspoken words and unresolved emotions. Every glance, every touch, every casual brush of hands carried a new layer of meaning. It was both exhilarating and painful, a reminder that life rarely unfolded in simple, straightforward ways.

That night, I lay awake in my room, replaying the conversation over and over in my mind. I thought about the way she had looked at me, the way her voice had wavered, and the sincerity in her voice. I realized that my feelings for her hadn't diminished; they had only grown stronger. And I also learned that love was rarely simple. Sometimes, it required patience, understanding, and a willingness to wait for the right moment.

In the weeks that followed, our friendship continued, tinged now with an awareness of what could be. We laughed together, studied together, and shared moments that felt intimate yet carefully bounded by the reality of her situation. Every interaction carried a quiet tension, an unspoken acknowledgment of the connection simmering beneath the surface.

And yet, in my heart, I knew one thing with certainty: no matter how long it took, no matter the obstacles, I was not going to let go of what we had begun.

Because some connections, once felt, cannot be ignored, cannot be forgotten, and are destined to find their way, even though the most unexpected turns.

CHAPTER SEVEN
The Distance Between Us

After my conversation with Deborah, I resolved to focus all my energy on my studies. That was the reason I had come to the United States, nothing more. I repeated that truth to myself like a quiet vow, especially in moments when my thoughts threatened to wander. I spent nearly all my time in the library, immersing myself in textbooks, lecture notes, and long hours of review, deliberately avoiding distractions. Discipline became my anchor. The structure of studying, reading, underlining, rewriting notes, gave me a sense of control in a season where my emotions felt less predictable.

As the school's Thanksgiving break approached, Deborah mentioned one day after class that she would be traveling to Mississippi to spend the holiday with her grandmother. She said it casually, as if it were just another detail of her plans, but I noticed a warmth in her voice when she spoke about her family. I nodded, wished her a safe trip, and told myself her absence would be good for me. While she was away, I buried myself even deeper in my studies, using the quiet days to recommit fully to my academic goals. I treated the break as an opportunity to work harder, to sharpen my focus, to remind myself why I had crossed an ocean in pursuit of an education.

School breaks were usually quiet for me. I didn't travel or go home; instead, I stayed on campus while many of the students dispersed. Those weeks were for catching up on reading, strengthening the subjects I struggled with, and reinforcing the purpose that had brought me to the United States in the first place. The library became my refuge during those slow days. Its silence steadied me. The muted footsteps, the occasional turning of a page, the hum of fluorescent lights overhead, all of it created a rhythm that calmed my mind and reminded me of my direction. In that stillness, I felt grounded.

Deborah had gone to visit her grandmother for the break. She had told me she would, yet I hadn't expected her absence to feel so noticeable. The campus felt different without her. Her laughter no longer echoed across the yard. Her quick greetings between classes, those brief moments of warmth, were missing from my days. I tried not to think about it too much. I reminded myself that I had not come to America to be distracted, not to lose myself in matters of the heart. I had come to pursue a dream built on sacrifice and determination.

And yet, despite my best efforts, there were moments when my discipline faltered. Sometimes, without warning, I caught myself wondering when she would return.

One afternoon, as I sat in my usual spot near the large window in the library, my biology book open, notes spread neatly around me, I sensed movement beside my table. It was subtle, just a presence entering my awareness. I looked up.

There she was.

Deborah.

For a brief second, the world seemed to pause. Her smile came before her words, bright, warm, and familiar, as though it carried the sunlight from wherever she had been.

"Mark," she said, her voice soft but full of excitement, "you're still here studying as always."

I smiled back, more easily than I expected. "Someone has to keep the library open."

She laughed, a delicate sound that immediately softened something inside me, something I had been holding tightly in place.

"May I sit?" she asked.

I nodded, and she pulled out the chair across from me, settling into it as though it were the most natural thing in the world. For a moment, she didn't say anything. She simply looked at me, her expression unreadable, gentle, thoughtful, and perhaps even grateful. There was a quiet between us that felt heavier than words.

"How was your trip?" I asked.

"It was... good," she said, pausing briefly, as if she

were choosing her words with care. "Different. Needed, I guess."

Her tone suggested there was more beneath the surface, but I didn't ask. Deborah had her own pace when it came to sharing personal things, and I respected that. We sat there in the library's calm hush, the familiarity between us unspoken yet unmistakable.

After that day, she started coming to the library more often than usual. Sometimes she would sit quietly nearby, working on her own assignments. Other times, she would stop just to say hello, ask how my studies were going, or share something small about her day. I sensed that she felt the distance I was trying to maintain, even if neither of us named it. Perhaps she was testing the space between us, or perhaps she wanted to remain connected in the only way she knew how.

As for me, I kept my focus on my studies. I told myself that was all I wanted, to concentrate, to succeed, to honor the sacrifices that had brought me here. Still, her presence lingered, a gentle interruption in my carefully guarded routine.

As the fall semester drew to a close, the campus grew busy again. Students crowded the library, preparing for final exams. Stress hung in the air, mixed with determination and fatigue. I studied relentlessly, moving from one subject to the next, pushing myself through long nights and early mornings. When final exams were over, the semester slowly wound down, and the campus prepared for Christmas break.

Deborah went home for the Christmas holiday. I stayed behind. While others traveled to be with family, I spent the holiday break working to make ends meet. My days were divided between long hours of labor and quiet nights of reflection. There were moments of loneliness, moments when the silence felt heavier than it had before. Yet I reminded myself again and again that this was part of the journey. Sacrifice was not new to me; it was familiar, almost expected.

Still, somewhere between work shifts and empty evenings, Deborah crossed my mind. Not as a distraction, I told myself, but as a quiet presence, one that lingered, patient and unresolved, waiting for a moment I had not yet allowed myself to acknowledge.

CHAPTER EIGHT
After Christmas Break

During the Christmas break, I ran into a schoolmate who told me the taxi company he worked for was hiring drivers. "I can introduce you to the supervisors if you want," he said. I didn't hesitate. Within days, I had my first job as a taxi driver, earning a few extra bucks. A week later, the same friend connected me with the supervisor at a security company where he worked a couple of times a week. I followed up and landed a second job as a security guard. The two jobs kept me busy, but I saw them as a way to cover my expenses, so I spent the entire break working.

When classes resumed, the struggle to balance school and work hit me right away. At first, it felt like walking a tightrope; I didn't want to give up either job. Gradually, I found a rhythm that let me manage both. I spent long hours in the library to stay ahead, burying myself in books whenever I could steal a moment.

One afternoon, as I was lost in a stack of notes, I heard the soft shuffle of footsteps behind me. Glancing up, I saw her, Deborah.

"Hey, Mark," she said, her voice light but warm.

"Hello, Deborah," I replied, smiling.

I asked, almost instinctively, "How was your Christmas break?"

"It was nice," she said, and then paused, as if deciding whether to linger. She pulled up a chair across from me, and we slipped into easy conversation. She laughed when I told her about juggling two jobs while going to school full-time, the sound bright in the quiet of the library. For a moment, it felt like the holidays had followed us into January, bringing a brief warmth to the routine of classes and work.

Then, after a brief silence, she folded her hands on the table and looked directly at me.

"Mark," she began, "I wanted to tell you something."

I closed my textbook slowly, giving her my full attention.

She took a deep breath, steadying, the kind someone takes right before saying something important. "I'm single now," she said quietly. "My boyfriend and I... we broke up."

Her voice didn't waver, but her eyes revealed a mixture of relief and lingering sadness. It wasn't easy news for her to share, and I knew that. I respected it.

I nodded gently. "I'm sorry to hear that."

She looked surprised, not at my words, but at my tone. Maybe she expected excitement, or questions, or some signal that I had been waiting for this moment. But the truth was, I hadn't.

I had been guarding my heart carefully, focusing on my studies, reminding myself that I was thousands of miles from home with a mission to fulfill. The last thing I wanted was to complicate my life or lose sight of why I was here.

"I just thought you should know," she said, her voice softening.

I nodded again, thoughtful. "Thank you for telling me."

She waited, as if she expected me to say something more, something more profound. But I stayed quiet. Not cold, not distant, just… steady.

The silence between us stretched, not uncomfortable, but filled with unspoken meaning. She studied my face for a moment, her eyes searching for something, maybe interest, maybe reassurance, maybe hope. But I had nothing more to offer at that moment.

I finally spoke, choosing my words carefully. "Deborah… I'm really focused on my studies right now. That's why I'm here."

She smiled, not hurt, not offended, but understanding. "I know," she said gently. "And that's one of the things I admire about you."

The word admires lingered in the air, warm and unexpected. She then reached for her bag and stood.

"Well," she said with a small smile, "I'll let you get back to studying. I didn't mean to interrupt."

"You're never interrupting," I replied. "It's always good to see you."

Her smile deepened, soft and genuine. "It's good to see you, too."

As she walked away, her footsteps quiet against the library tiles, I watched her go, feeling something shift in the space between us. Something unique, something real. She was available now.

But I wasn't ready.

Not yet.

And so, without saying it aloud, I tucked my heart back into the pages of my books, convincing myself that my education came first.

But destiny had other plans.

It always does.

CHAPTER NINE
The Quiet Pull Between Us

After Deborah left the library that day, I tried to return to my notes, but the words on the page blurred into meaninglessness. Lines I had read a hundred times before now refused to settle in my mind. My pen hovered uselessly above the paper, as if it, too, was uncertain of its purpose. My thoughts were no longer mine to command; they drifted back to her with a quiet insistence, replaying our conversation over and over, her honesty, unguarded and sincere; the way her eyes searched mine as though she were looking not just for understanding, but for reassurance; the softening of her voice when she said she was glad we met.

It felt as though a door had swung open inside me, one I hadn't known existed, and behind it stretched a vast, uncharted world. I stood at its threshold, aware of its presence but unsure whether I dared to step through. That door led somewhere deeper than reason or intention. It led into a part of myself I had kept sealed since leaving Nigeria, a part shaped by longing, restraint, and a determination to survive first, to feel later.

I gathered my books slowly, moving through the familiar motions as if they belonged to someone else. The library, usually a place of order and refuge, felt strangely altered, as though it had witnessed something intimate and was now quietly holding the secret. As I stepped outside, the afternoon sun warmed my face, but my thoughts remained inward, circling the same questions without answers.

What had just happened? And why did it feel like the beginning of something I could neither predict nor prevent?

Over the next few days, campus life resumed its usual rhythm. Students hurried across the yard with books pressed to their chests, their conversations overlapping in bursts of laughter and complaint. Friends gathered under the shade of live oaks, stretched out on the grass, debating weekend plans or lingering over stories that seemed urgent only in that moment. Somewhere on the breeze was the warm, steady hum of New Orleans itself, a city alive even in its quietest moments. Music drifted faintly from a nearby dorm window.

Life moved forward, unconcerned with the quiet shift that had taken place inside me. But now, intertwined into that everyday rhythm, was Deborah.

Before We Understood

Every class we shared became a delicate dance of glances and quiet greetings. She would slide into her seat, her smile small but warm, the kind that made you forget the rest of the room existed. Sometimes she whispered a quick "Good morning," her voice low and intimate, meant only for me. Other times, she nodded with a shy confidence that made my heart shift in my chest. Those brief moments, no more than a second or two, held a weight disproportionate to their simplicity. They lingered with me long after the lecture ended.

I became acutely aware of her presence in ways I couldn't explain. The sound of her turning a page. The thoughtful crease that appeared between her brows when she concentrated. The way she tilted her head slightly when listening, as if fully committing herself to the moment. These were not grand gestures or dramatic scenes; they were quiet details, easily overlooked by anyone else. Yet to me, they carried a significance that felt almost sacred.

Our conversations grew gradually, small exchanges at first. A homework question. A comment about the lab assignment. A shared laugh at something the professor said. We spoke the language of students, practical and measured, but beneath it ran an unspoken undercurrent. Each conversation felt like a step closer, though neither of us named the direction we were heading.

Between classes, I found myself anticipating those moments more than I cared to admit. I would arrive early, choosing a seat where I could see the doorway, telling myself it was a coincidence even as I waited. When she appeared, there was always that brief instant, just a flicker, where our eyes met, and something passed between us that words could not contain.

At night, alone in my room, I tried to reason with myself. I reminded myself why I was here. I had come to the United States with a singular purpose: education. Survival. Building a future that had once felt impossibly distant. I had crossed oceans, left behind family, familiarity, and the rhythm of life I had known in Nigeria. I had promised myself that distractions would not derail me. Feelings, I believed, could wait.

So far, the feelings I was learning do not wait politely for permission.

Memories of my life before this moment surfaced uninvited. I thought of Nigeria, the heat, the voices, the sense of belonging that came from shared history and culture. I remembered the weight of expectation, the responsibility I carried as a son, as a young man tasked with making something of himself. Leaving had not been an escape; it had been a gamble, fueled by hope and necessity.

In those early months in America, loneliness had been my constant companion, even when surrounded by people. I had learned to move through my days with focus and discipline, keeping my heart guarded, my attention fixed on the path ahead.

And now Deborah had appeared, quietly, without force or demand, unsettling the careful order I had constructed.

Sometimes we studied together in the library, sitting across from each other in companionable silence. Our books lay open, notes spread out, but there were moments when I would glance up and catch her looking at me, a faint smile playing at the corners of her mouth.

We never lingered too long in those moments. One of us would look away, returning to the task at hand, as if acknowledging too much would break something fragile.

Other times, we walked together after class, our steps naturally falling into sync. We talked about ordinary things, assignments, upcoming exams, the weather, and the quirks of campus life. Yet even then, there was an ease between us that felt rare, as though we had known each other longer than we actually had. Silence never felt awkward. It felt shared.

I began to notice how she spoke of her own life, carefully but honestly. She didn't overshare, yet when she did say, there was a depth to her words, a thoughtfulness that drew me in. I sensed that she, too, carried her own history of choices and consequences, of hope tempered by experience. There was strength in her, quiet and steady, the kind that doesn't announce itself.

One afternoon, as we stood beneath the shade of a large oak tree, she spoke about her family. Her voice softened, her gaze distant, as if she were seeing them in her mind. I listened, truly listened, not just to her words but to the emotions beneath them. In that moment, I felt a shift, an awareness that this was no longer simply a friendship of convenience or proximity. Something deeper was taking root.

Deep inside, I felt something whisper that destiny had just spoken in the quiet of those classroom days before, and it was continuing its conversation now, patiently, persistently.

Still, I resisted. I told myself that feelings were fleeting, that what I felt was simply gratitude for connection in a foreign place. I buried myself in my studies, spending long hours in the library, convincing myself that discipline could override emotion. Yet even there, surrounded by books and silence, Deborah found her way into my thoughts. I would read a passage and realize I hadn't absorbed a single word, my mind wandering back to her smile, her voice, the way she listened.

For the first time since leaving Nigeria, I felt something shift at the core of my journey. I had believed this path was about education alone, about rebuilding my future one class, one exam at a time. That had been the story I told myself, the safe story, the manageable one. But now I sensed that my journey was about to transform into something far more profound.

It wasn't just about where I was going, but about who I was becoming.

There were moments of fear in that realization. To care was to risk distraction. To open my heart was to invite vulnerability. I had worked too hard, sacrificed too much, to lose focus now. And yet, there was also a quiet joy, a sense of alignment, as though something long dormant within me was finally being acknowledged.

Deborah never pressured me, never demanded clarity or declaration. That, too, was part of what drew me to her. She allowed space, respected boundaries, and remained present. Her presence was steady, not overwhelming, and in that steadiness, I found myself slowly letting my guard down.

Before We Understood

Weeks passed, marked by exams, deadlines, and the subtle deepening of our connection. We shared small victories, good grades, completed projects, and offered encouragement during stressful moments. There was comfort in knowing that someone saw you, understood the weight you carried, without needing explanation.

One evening, after a long day of classes, we sat together as the sun dipped below the horizon, painting the sky in shades of orange and purple. Neither of us spoke for a while. The campus around us quieted, the daytime energy giving way to something softer. In that silence, I felt an overwhelming sense of gratitude, not just for Deborah, but for the path that had led me here, for the unseen forces that had guided our lives to intersect.

I realized then that some stories do not begin with dramatic declarations or sudden confessions. Some begin quietly, in shared glances and unspoken understanding, in the gentle unfolding of trust. They start before you fully recognize them, choosing you long before you choose them.

And so, without fully understanding it, I stepped closer to that open door within me. I didn't rush through it. I didn't name what lay beyond. I allowed myself to stand there, acknowledging its presence, feeling its pull.

For the first time since leaving Nigeria, I no longer felt that my life was divided between past and future, sacrifice and reward. Instead, it felt as though all those pieces were beginning to converge, forming something whole.

A story had begun.

A story neither of us yet understood.

A story that had already chosen us.

CHAPTER TEN
Destiny Doesn't Rush

As time passed, our friendship deepened into something stable yet electric, gentle yet intense. It was a bond built not on declarations or promises but on shared moments, easy laughter, quiet conversations, and the unmistakable warmth of two people whose lives had begun to intertwine long before they understood why.

But fate, ever patient, was still working in silence.

Guiding.

Shaping.

Waiting.

I didn't know then that love can begin softly, like a whisper that it can root itself in small moments, a smile, a shared book, a walk to class, long before the heart dares to speak its truth.

Before We Understood

All I knew was that Deborah was becoming part of my world in ways I never expected. And somewhere deep down, beneath the caution and the boundaries and the unspoken emotions, I sensed that the story between us was only beginning.

It was the kind of closeness that didn't need labels, the kind of understanding that arrived in glances, in the subtle ways we found each other in a crowded room, or in a library where our hands would accidentally brush over the same textbook.

There was a beat to our friendship, a steady tempo that felt both comforting and exhilarating. We didn't rush. There was no forceful urgency in our interactions. No dramatic confessions or grand gestures. Instead, our connection grew in silence and in the smallest of ways: a shared joke that lingered longer than expected, a nod of understanding when words failed, a cup of tea shared in the nearby Chinese restaurant. These moments seemed ordinary, yet in retrospect, they were anything but; they were the scaffolding upon which something extraordinary was slowly being built.

I didn't fully realize it at the time, but destiny has its own pace. It doesn't knock on your door or demand your attention. It doesn't come wrapped in clarity or certainty. It moves quietly, nudging people together, aligning paths, and setting the stage for what is meant to unfold. In our case, fate was patient, deliberate, and gentle.

It worked in the spaces between our conversations, in the laughter we shared, and in the silences we sat through without discomfort. It was shaping the story we had yet to recognize, laying the groundwork for a bond that would eventually transform into something neither of us could have anticipated.

I remember the first time I noticed it, the delicate shift in how I thought about her. Not the obvious things, not the dazzling smile or the easy way she could make anyone feel at ease, but the quiet consistency of her presence. Deborah had a way of appearing in moments I didn't expect, of leaving impressions that lingered long after she had gone. She would offer insights on things I hadn't yet considered, laugh at jokes I didn't know I needed, and always, always make the ordinary feel extraordinary. I realized slowly, almost imperceptibly, that she was becoming an integral part of my world.

It wasn't immediate. Love, as I would later come to understand, doesn't always announce itself with fireworks and sudden clarity. Sometimes, it begins softly, almost imperceptibly. A glance that lasts a fraction too long, a conversation that leaves you thinking hours afterward, a simple act of kindness that resonates deeper than the moment itself. These were the moments that began to plant the seed of something far greater. And for me, those seeds were quietly taking root.

Even as the connection deepened, there were boundaries. There was an unspoken understanding between us that neither of us was ready to cross. Life had its complications, previous relationships, personal ambitions, and uncertainties about the future. And so we stayed within the safe confines of friendship, navigating the delicate balance of closeness without overstepping, of intimacy without expectation. We shared pieces of ourselves, fragments of our lives, while holding back the parts that might make us vulnerable in ways we were not yet prepared to confront.

Despite this caution, the energy between us was undeniable. There was a tension that existed quietly, our interactions that hinted at something more, something neither of us dared to name. It lived in the way our conversations would linger longer than necessary, in the accidental brushes of hands that sent a brief shiver through the air, in the way our eyes sometimes met and held each other's gaze a second too long. These were subtle signs, easily dismissed as a coincidence, yet they carried a weight that could not be ignored.

And all the while, fate continued its quiet work. It doesn't hurry. It doesn't demand. It moves in whispers, not shouts, in gentle nudges rather than overt commands. I did not realize at the time how deliberate it was, how carefully it was guiding us toward a moment we could not yet foresee. Every encounter, every shared laugh, every brief exchange was a brushstroke on a canvas we could not yet comprehend, a painting that would only reveal its full image in due course.

I often reflect on the patience required in those early months. There was a certain beauty in not knowing, in letting things unfold organically, in resisting the temptation to rush or to force clarity where none existed. It was in those pauses, those quiet intervals, that the deepest bonds were forming. Our connection was like a river, flowing steadily beneath the surface, carving its path through unseen terrain. And, like a river, it was unstoppable, moving silently yet with relentless purpose, eventually finding the path that would lead it into the light.

There were times when I questioned myself, wondering whether I was misreading the signs, whether I was attaching meaning where none existed. But each time I doubted, something would remind me of the depth of our connection. A smile exchanged in passing, a shared memory that resurfaced unexpectedly, the effortless way our conversations picked up exactly where they left off, no matter how much time had passed. In those moments, I realized our bond was not accidental. It was intentional, deliberate in its quiet way, a product of timing and circumstance working together with something larger than either of us could fully comprehend.

Deborah, unknowingly, became a mirror in which I could see aspects of myself I had not recognized. She reflected my own hopes and insecurities, my aspirations, and fears, in a way that was both comforting and unsettling. In her presence, I discovered a clarity of thought, a depth of reflection, and a capacity for understanding that I had not known I possessed. She had a way of listening that made you feel truly seen, in a rare and precious way. And slowly, imperceptibly, I found that my thoughts often drifted toward her, not in a frantic or desperate way, but in a quiet, contemplative manner, as if she were an inevitable part of the mental landscape I carried with me every day.

The quiet intensity of our friendship was something I came to cherish. There was a peace in knowing that I could share my thoughts with her without fear of judgment, that I could express doubts and dreams alike, and that she would meet them with a kind of understanding that transcended simple empathy. It was a connection rooted in trust, in mutual respect, and in the awareness that, though we were still learning about each other, the foundation we were building was strong and enduring.

Thus far, even as the bond deepened, life's unpredictability remained a constant companion. Plans changed, circumstances shifted, and external pressures often demanded attention. And in those moments of disruption, I realized how much I had come to rely on her presence, even in the smallest ways: checking in, a casual conversation, a shared joke that cut through the monotony of a difficult day. The constancy of her being was a reminder that some connections are meant to endure, even when the world around them is in flux.

I began to understand that love, in its most valid form, is not always a dramatic declaration. It is often a quiet, persistent presence that infiltrates daily life in the most unassuming ways. It resides in shared glances and laughter, in the comfort of familiarity, in the knowledge that someone else holds a piece of your world with care and reverence. And it grows, slowly and deliberately, in the spaces between words, in the silences that speak louder than conversation ever could.

There was a lesson in all of this, a lesson about patience, about trust, and about the subtlety of fate. Destiny does not hurry. It does not announce itself with grandiose gestures or lightning bolts of clarity. It moves quietly, imperceptibly, shaping lives that are often invisible until the moment of revelation. And when it does, the culmination of all the quiet work that has been happening beneath the surface becomes impossible to ignore.

I didn't know then that what we were experiencing was love in its earliest, most delicate form. I didn't recognize it as such because it did not conform to the dramatic narratives I had seen in books or movies. It was softer, quieter, yet no less real. It was a love built on shared experiences, on understanding, on the unwavering presence of one soul in another's life. It was the kind of love that could survive uncertainty, navigate distance, and endure the pressures of life because it had been cultivated patiently, thoughtfully, and with care.

And somewhere deep down, beneath the caution and the boundaries and the unspoken emotions, I sensed that the story between us was only beginning. It was a story that would require patience, courage, and the willingness to embrace uncertainty. It was a story that would test and challenge us, ultimately revealing the depth of what we could mean to each other. But I also sensed, with a quiet certainty, that it was a story worth waiting for, worth nurturing, and worth allowing to unfold in its own time.

Looking back, I can see how every seemingly insignificant moment, the brief laughter, the accidental touches, the shared silences, was part of the larger narrative being written by forces beyond our immediate understanding. I can see how destiny was at work, moving quietly, deliberately, ensuring that when the time was right, we would recognize the full measure of our connection. And I understand now that the patience required in those early days was not a limitation, but a gift that allowed love to grow in its most authentic and enduring form.

In the end, destiny doesn't rush. It doesn't need to. Its power lies in its subtlety, quiet persistence, and ability to shape lives without drawing attention to itself. And sometimes, the greatest love stories are not those that explode into existence, but those that unfold gradually, beautifully, and with a depth that can only be achieved through patience, trust, and the gentle guidance of fate.

Deborah became more than a friend. She became part of my world, a presence that colored my thoughts, influenced my choices, and shaped how I saw life. And though I could not have known it at the time, she was also the beginning of a story that would transform everything, quietly, deliberately, and in ways that only destiny could orchestrate.

CHAPTER ELEVEN
Destiny Moves Quietly

Love, I learned, rarely announces itself. It does not arrive with fanfare or demand recognition the moment it enters our lives. Instead, it moves quietly, settling into ordinary days and unremarkable moments, growing slowly in patience and restraint. It takes shape in shared silences, in gentle understanding, and in the steady presence of another person who lingers longer than expected. Only in hindsight do we recognize its careful work, realizing that what once felt small or incidental was destiny unfolding, deliberate, unhurried, and certain.

At the time, our story was only beginning. It had not yet found its rhythm or revealed its direction, but even in those early chapters, it carried the unmistakable imprint of something enduring. There was a quiet gravity to it, something rare and steady, something that did not demand attention yet refused to be ignored. It felt unhurried, as though it understood that meaning deepens when it is given room to breathe. That, I came to understand, was the true magic of destiny. It does not rush to prove itself. It moves quietly, yes, but with certainty, guiding hearts that are ready to meet, shaping lives that are prepared to intertwine, and reminding us that the most meaningful journeys are never hurried. They are deliberate, unfolding at precisely the pace they are meant to.

While these realizations slowly formed within me, life continued to demand practical decisions. Dreams and emotions, no matter how powerful, still had to coexist with responsibility. I decided to move off campus, not because I wanted to distance myself from the university community, but because it was the most sensible choice at the time. My financial resources were limited, and continuing my education required careful planning and sacrifice. The cost of room and board weighed heavily on me, and I knew that if I wanted to remain enrolled and avoid accumulating unnecessary debt, I would have to adjust.

The decision was not easy. Leaving campus meant surrendering convenience, structure, and a sense of belonging that came with living among other students. It meant trading late-night conversations in dorm hallways for quieter evenings alone, and familiar routines for new ones that required greater discipline. Still, practicality demanded courage of its own. I reminded myself that this move was not a step backward, but a strategic decision, one rooted in foresight and responsibility. By lowering my living expenses, I could save more of my earnings and apply them toward paying my tuition for the upcoming semester. It was a necessary sacrifice; one made in service of a longer-term goal.

To support this plan, I purchased a used silver 1980 compact Subaru. It was neither flashy nor new, but it represented something far more valuable to me than appearances: independence. With the car, I could commute between work and school without relying on public transportation or others' generosity. I could manage my time more effectively, take on additional responsibilities, and move through my days with greater flexibility. The car became a symbol of self-reliance and quiet progress, proof that I was taking control of my circumstances rather than letting them dictate my future.

For a while, everything seemed to align. I settled into my new routine, balancing work, classes, and long hours of study. There was exhaustion, certainly, but also a deep sense of purpose. Each day felt intentional, each sacrifice justified by the promise of something better ahead. I told myself that this was what perseverance looked like, not dramatic triumphs, but steady forward motion.

Then life intervened, as it often does, without warning or apology. I was involved in a car accident. In an instant, the sense of stability I had worked so carefully to build felt threatened. The accident itself was jarring, but what followed weighed even heavier: the financial strain, the disruption to my routine, the fear that this setback might derail my carefully constructed plans. For a brief moment, I allowed myself to feel overwhelmed. I questioned whether I was pushing myself too hard, whether the sacrifices were worth the cost.

Even in that moment of uncertainty, I refused to give in to despair. I reminded myself of why I had come so far and what I was working toward. With determination and persistence, I managed to replace the vehicle. It was not easy and required further sacrifice, but it allowed me to keep moving forward. The experience taught me a quiet yet enduring lesson: setbacks are inevitable, but they need not define the journey. They are interruptions, not endings, tests of resolve rather than signs of failure.

Life resumed its rhythm, altered but intact. I returned to my studies with renewed focus, aware now that progress is rarely linear. It bends, falters, and resumes, shaped by resilience rather than perfection. It was during this period, one marked by introspection and careful rebuilding, that an unexpected moment quietly reminded me of the emotional thread still weaving through my life.

One afternoon, while I was studying in the library, Deborah passed by. The library had become a familiar refuge for me, a place where time seemed to slow, and distractions faded into the background. Surrounded by shelves of books and the soft murmur of turning pages, I was deeply immersed in my studies when I noticed her presence. She paused when she saw me and stopped to say hello.

"Hi Mark," She said

"Hey Deborah," I responded

"I don't mean to interrupt your studying," she said. "I'm just passing by," she continued.

"Okay. See you around," I said.

By then, a noticeable distance had grown between us. Time, circumstances, and unspoken complexities had shifted the dynamic we once shared. We were no longer as close as we had been, and that distance lingered quietly between us, unacknowledged yet unmistakable. Still, her voice carried a warmth that felt familiar, echoing a connection that had never fully disappeared.

Our conversation was brief, almost casual, yet layered with meaning. She turned to leave, but after a few steps, she turned around and came back.

"Can we talk for a few minutes?" she asked.

"Certainly," I said.

"How are you?" she asked.

"Well, I am fine," I replied. "I had an accident with my Subaru. I'm not hurt, just a bit shaken. I did get another car, a red and silver 1981 Dodge Challenger," I continued.

She listened attentively, her expression softening with genuine concern. She expressed sympathy for what had happened, her words gentle and sincere. Then, with a slight smile that carried both ease and intention, she added that she would like to ride in my new car someday.

The words themselves were simple, but their impact lingered long after she walked away. In that moment, I was reminded once again of how destiny operates, not through grand declarations or dramatic reunions, but through small, meaningful exchanges that leave a lasting impression. Even in distance, even after change, something remained unspoken yet undeniable. It was not a return to what had been, nor a promise of what would be, but a quiet acknowledgment of connection.

Before We Understood

As I sat there afterward, the weight of the moment settled gently over me. It struck me how easily such moments could be overlooked, dismissed as casual or insignificant. Still, I knew better by then. I had learned that meaning often reveals itself slowly, only to those willing to pay attention. Destiny, I realized, does not shout. It whispers. It places moments in our path and waits to see whether we are patient enough to recognize them.

Looking back now, I see how all these threads, love, sacrifice, loss, resilience, and quiet connection, were already weaving themselves together. My choices to move off campus, to manage my finances carefully, to persist after setbacks were not separate from the emotional journey unfolding alongside them. They were part of the same process: becoming someone capable of endurance, responsibility, and depth.

In those days, I did not yet know where the path would lead or how the story would unfold. I only knew that something meaningful was taking shape, both within me and beyond me. Perhaps that is the essence of destiny, not clarity from the beginning but confidence in the unfolding. It is the understanding that the most important chapters are often written slowly, shaped by patience rather than haste.

Our story was still in its infancy, its direction uncertain, its ending unknown. But even then, it carried the unmistakable mark of something enduring, something rare, something that refused to be rushed. And that, I came to understand, was destiny in its truest form: quiet, deliberate, and unwavering, guiding hearts and shaping lives with a certainty that needed no announcement.

CHAPTER TWELVE
Even in the Distance

Distance has a way of clarifying what closeness sometimes obscures. When people drift apart, not through conflict, but through circumstance, the silence between them becomes a mirror. It reflects what mattered, what endured, and what was never as fragile as it once seemed. After that brief encounter in the library, I carried Deborah's words with me longer than I expected. They were simple, almost casual, yet they lingered in my thoughts with a quiet persistence. It wasn't what she said so much as how she said it, the warmth that remained, even after time and distance, had reshaped our connection.

Life, however, did not pause to allow me the luxury of introspection. Responsibilities pressed in from every side. My days became tightly scheduled, divided between work, classes, and long evenings of study. I spent countless hours in the library, not only because it was conducive to focus, but because it offered a kind of refuge. There, surrounded by books and silence, I felt temporarily insulated from the future's uncertainty. Each page I read, each concept I mastered, felt like a small act of defiance against the instability that had marked so much of my journey.

Even as I immersed myself in academic discipline, my thoughts occasionally wandered back to Deborah. Not in a disruptive way, but gently, like a memory passing through. I wondered how she was doing, what occupied her days, and whether she felt the same sense of unfinished connection I did. There was no urgency to these thoughts, no longing that demanded resolution. Instead, there was acceptance, an understanding that some connections do not fade simply because they are no longer foregrounded in our lives.

The weeks that followed were marked by steady progress and quiet endurance. I adapted to my off-campus life, learning to manage expenses with precision and to stretch every dollar as far as possible. There were moments of exhaustion, days when the weight of responsibility felt heavy, but there was also pride. Each sacrifice reinforced my sense of purpose. I was not merely surviving; I was building something, piece by piece.

Occasionally, our paths crossed in passing, brief glimpses in hallways or shared spaces where words were unnecessary and perhaps even unwelcome. When our eyes met, there was always mutual recognition, a silent acknowledgment that what we shared had not been erased by time. It still existed, transformed but intact, as a familiar melody heard at a distance.

One afternoon, weeks after our conversation in the library, I saw Deborah again, this time across a crowded campus walkway. She was laughing with a friend, her expression unguarded and light. For a moment, I considered approaching her, offering a greeting more intentionally than a passing nod. But something held me back. It wasn't fear or hesitation, but respect, for the moment, for the space between us, for the understanding that not every connection needs to be immediately reentered.

That restraint, I realized, was something I had learned over time. Earlier in my life, I might have rushed forward, eager to reclaim what felt familiar. But growth had taught me the value of patience, the wisdom of allowing things to unfold without force. If destiny had taught me anything, it was that timing matters, not just in love, but in life itself.

As the spring semester progressed, my focus sharpened. I found myself more disciplined, more deliberate in how I approached both my studies and my relationships. There was less room for distraction, but more space for clarity. I began to understand that becoming ready, for love, for opportunity, for the future, was not about waiting passively, but about preparing actively. It was about becoming someone capable of sustaining what might one day arrive.

There were nights when I sat alone in my small

apartment, the silence broken only by the sound of passing trains behind my apartment building. In those moments, solitude no longer felt like absence. It felt like grounding. I reflected on how far I had come, from uncertainty to intention, from reaction to resolve. And in that stillness, I felt a growing sense of peace.

Deborah remained part of my inner landscape, not as a source of longing, but as a muted presence, one that reminded me of the kind of connection that is not diminished by distance. She represented a chapter not yet closed, a possibility that had not expired simply because it had paused. I did not know whether our paths would converge again, or in what form. But I trusted, perhaps for the first time fully, that whatever was meant to endure would find its way.

In the end, distance did not weaken the story; it refined it. It stripped away assumptions and replaced them with understanding. It taught me that some bonds are not measured by proximity but by continuity, by how they persist without demand.

And so, I moved forward, grounded in my purpose, attentive to my responsibilities, and open, pleasantly to whatever the next chapter would bring. Destiny, I knew by then, was still at work. It always was. Not loudly, not urgently, but faithfully moving even in the distance.

CHAPTER THIRTEEN
Unspoken Connection

Our connection did not surge forward with urgency or expectation. It expanded the way morning light does gradually, almost imperceptibly, until suddenly the room is full. We began to spend more time together without ever formally deciding to do so. It simply happened. A seat saved in class. A shared walk after lectures. Study sessions that started with intention and dissolved into conversation.

There was something grounding about its predictability. We were not chasing moments; we were inhabiting them.

I learned her habits in fragments. She liked quiet mornings and needed time before words came easily. She focused best with soft background noise, never complete silence. She had a habit of raising her eyebrows when she was thinking. These details were never announced. They revealed themselves slowly, the way trust does.

In return, she learned me.

She learned that I am quiet with few words, that I talked more when I get to know someone a little better, that I carried responsibility like something fragile, carefully, sometimes too carefully. She learned that I questioned myself often, replayed conversations long after they ended, and measured my worth in effort more than outcome. And instead of trying to correct any of it, she simply made room for it.

There was relief in that.

One afternoon, while studying together, she asked me a simple question: "Do you ever let yourself rest?"

The question caught me off guard not because it was invasive, but because it was accurate. I laughed it off at first, deflecting with humor, but she did not press. She didn't need to. The question lingered quietly, settling somewhere deeper than I expected. Being with her had a way of revealing truths without confrontation.

As time passed, the line between friendship and something more grew less ambiguous, though it remained unnamed. There were moments of closeness that felt intentional: sitting a little nearer than necessary, hands brushing without retreat, shared looks that held longer than coincidence would allow. None of it felt rushed. If anything, it felt careful, as though we were both aware that what was forming deserved patience.

I noticed how attuned she was to emotional shifts

not just mine, but others. She listened with her whole body, leaning in slightly, eyes steady, never interrupting. When she spoke, it was measured, thoughtful, as if she believed words should earn their place. That kind of presence was rare. It made people feel safe. It made me feel safe.

Still, uncertainty did not disappear. There were moments when I wondered whether I was misreading things, whether the ease I felt was shared or imagined. I carried those doubts quietly, afraid that naming them might disturb the balance we had found. I had learned, through experience, that too much pressure too soon could fracture something fragile. So, I waited. And she did too, though I didn't fully understand that until later.

One evening, as we walked across campus under a sky heavy with clouds, the conversation drifted into silence. Not the comfortable kind, this one had weight. We slowed our steps without realizing it, both sensing that something unspoken was pressing forward.

"I've been thinking about us," she said finally, her voice calm but deliberate.

My heart quickened, not from fear, but from recognition. This moment had been approaching, quietly, patiently.

"So have I," I admitted.

She stopped walking and turned to face me. There was no drama in her expression, no guardedness. Just honesty. "I like what this is," she said. "And I don't want to rush it. But I also do not want to pretend it doesn't matter."

The simplicity of her words disarmed me. There was

no demand, no expectation, only clarity.

"It matters to me," I said. "More than I've been letting on."

She smiled then, not brightly, but warmly. The kind of smile that settles rather than excites.

That conversation did not change our pace. It didn't redefine our routines or introduce new labels. But it anchored something between us. It gave our connection a shared awareness, a mutual acknowledgment that what we were building was intentional, even if it remained unhurried.

From that point on, the world felt slightly more aligned. We moved with greater confidence in each other's presence. There was less second-guessing, less internal negotiation. We allowed ourselves to enjoy what was unfolding without constantly questioning its legitimacy.

I began to understand that intimacy is not always marked by grand moments. Often, it reveals itself in consistency, in choosing the same person again and again, even when nothing spectacular is happening. Especially then.

Looking back, I see that this chapter of our story was about learning how to stay. Not in the sense of permanence, but in presence. Learning how to show up honestly, without performance or pretense. Learning that connection deepens not through acceleration, but through attention.

We were not racing toward a future. We were inhabiting a present that felt steady and real. And for the first time in a long while, that felt like enough.

CHAPTER FOURTEEN
When Quiet Becomes Certain

There is a moment in every unfolding connection when uncertainty loosens its grip. It does not vanish completely, doubt is too deeply human for that, but it no longer dominates every thought. For us, that moment did not arrive with a declaration or a dramatic shift. It came softly, through repetition, through the steady accumulation of ordinary days that began to feel essential rather than incidental.

We had slipped into a rhythm so natural that neither of us thought to question it. She was intertwined in my life in ways no planner or syllabus could account for. I did not schedule time with her; it simply existed. I expected her presence without demanding it, and she offered it without obligation. And somewhere along the way, her absence became noticeable, not in a way that caused anxiety, but in the way one notices when a familiar sound is missing from the background. The day still went on, but something felt off.

That realization startled me, not because it frightened me but because it clarified something I had been circling without naming.

One evening made that clarity unavoidable. It was late, the kind of late that thins the world to essentials. We sat together in the campus library, long past its busiest hours. Most tables were empty now, with abandoned books stacked neatly, as if their owners planned to return but never did. The silence felt deliberate, almost protective. The air carried the scent of paper, dust, and quiet perseverance.

Our books lay open in front of us, but neither of us was reading. We spoke softly, mindful of the stillness around us. Not about anything urgent or profound. We talked about how tired we were, how the semester seemed to accelerate without warning. About how strange it felt to carry so many responsibilities while, unexpectedly, feeling at peace.

At some point, without ceremony or hesitation, she leaned her head against my shoulder.

The gesture was simple, almost casual. But it landed with a weight I hadn't anticipated.

I didn't move. I didn't speak. I became acutely aware of the warmth where she rested against me and of the quiet trust embedded in that small act. There was no question in it, no testing of boundaries. It wasn't tentative or charged. It was certain.

In that moment, something settled inside me. I understood, then, that intimacy does not always announce itself through urgency or intensity. Sometimes it arrives gently, without spectacle, and precisely because of that, it feels inevitable rather than chosen. It doesn't ask for permission. It simply takes its place.

After that night, physical closeness stopped feeling like something we were approaching and began to feel like something we were inhabiting. Our hands found each other naturally. Our proximity felt intentional, not calculated. We didn't ask, "Is this okay?" because the answer lived in our awareness of each other, in the care with which we moved, and the attention we paid to both spoken and unspoken cues.

Still, we were careful.

Not distant, not guarded, but intentional. We understood, even without saying it, that what was forming deserved respect. We talked openly, sometimes haltingly, about fears that had nothing to do with each other yet affected everything else. She spoke of the pressure to succeed, of expectations that followed her, shaping her decisions even when she tried to ignore them. I spoke of my relentless drive, of the fear of falling behind, of the uncertainty that came with building a future without a clear map.

These conversations didn't offer solutions. They weren't meant to. Instead, they offered understanding. And that understanding became a foundation.

There were moments of friction, small disagreements and misunderstandings born of fatigue or assumption.

What mattered was how we handled them. There was no retreat into silence, no punishment disguised as distance. We learned to pause, listen without rehearsing defenses, and admit when we were wrong without making it a confession. Repair became more important than being right.

Each time we navigated a moment like that, our trust deepened.

One night, as we walked back from a late study session, the campus was nearly empty around us, and she stopped beneath a streetlight. The glow softened her expression, yet a seriousness in her eyes felt different from before. This wasn't reflection or curiosity. It was an intention.

"I want to be clear about something," she said. "I'm not here casually."

The words settled between us, heavy with implication.

Commitment, not as a contract, not as a label, but as an intention, had entered the space. Not loudly. Not dramatically. But undeniably.

Neither was I.

"I know," I said. "I'm not either."

That was as close as we came to defining what we were, and it was enough. There was no pressure to formalize it, no need to anchor it with titles. The certainty lived elsewhere, in action, in consistency, in the way we made room for each other's lives.

From that point on, our connection revealed itself less in words and more in choices. In the way we considered each other when making decisions, even small ones. In the way we adjusted schedules without resentment. In the way our futures, still undefined and uncertain, began to feel adjacent rather than separate.

Looking back now, I understand how easily certainty can be mistaken for excitement and how often people chase intensity, believing it signals depth. What we had was quieter, steadier, and far more durable.

Indeed, I learned that it is not the absence of doubt. It is the willingness to remain present despite it. It is choosing to stay, not because everything is resolved, but because what is unresolved feels safer when faced together.

By then, staying didn't feel like a decision.

It felt natural.

It felt chosen.

CHAPTER FIFTEEN
A Way to Stay

The certainty we had reached did not insulate us from life. If anything, it sharpened our awareness of it. Responsibilities did not recede just because we had found steadiness in each other. Classes grew more demanding, deadlines clustered. Expectations, spoken and unspoken, pressed closer. But something fundamental had shifted in how I carried those pressures. They no longer felt like solitary weights. Even when she wasn't physically present, knowing her steadiness altered my posture toward everything else.

It became clear to me then that love, at least in its most valid form, does not remove difficulty. It rearranges it. What once felt heavy now felt shared, even though it remained mine to bear.

We did not mark this transition with a ceremony.

Before We Understood

There was no anniversary, no defining conversation, no moment when we looked at each other and acknowledged we had crossed into a new phase. Instead, it revealed itself in habit. In the way, she became the first person I looked for in a crowded room. In the way, I instinctively adjusted my plans, not out of obligation, but out of consideration.

She did the same. I noticed it in the small accommodations she made, the simple recalibrations that spoke louder than promises. The way she remembered details I had forgotten to mention. The way she checked in without prying. The way she respected my silences without mistaking them for distance.

I learned to say, "I'm overwhelmed," without apologizing. I learned that needing space didn't mean needing separation. I learned that vulnerability didn't make me less capable; it made me more connected. And each time I risked that openness, she met it with steadiness rather than alarm.

She had her own moments, too. Times when the pressure she carried surfaced unexpectedly, and her confidence wavered beneath expectations she rarely voiced aloud. In those moments, she did not ask me to fix anything. She did not want reassurance packaged as solutions. She wanted presence. Attention. The permission to feel what she felt without having to justify it.

We learned to sit with each other in discomfort. Not to rush it away. Not to frame it as something to overcome. Just to allow it to exist, knowing it would eventually pass.

That, I realized, was its own form of intimacy.

One afternoon remains vivid in my memory, not for its drama but for what it revealed about us. We had intended to study together, yet upon her arrival, it was obvious she was carrying more than just textbooks. Her motions were sluggish, and her focus was fragmented. I inquired about her well-being, and she paused briefly before saying she wasn't prepared to explain.

So, we didn't study. We sat instead, side by side, not touching, not speaking much. The afternoon passed in fragments: a few exchanged sentences, a shared glance, the quiet acknowledgment of each other's presence. When she finally spoke, hours later, her words came haltingly.

"My program of study is not really what I thought it would be," she said.

"What is the problem with your program?" I responded

She continued, "The classes offered are not in line with my future goals. I may have to transfer to another university, but I have not yet made that decision."

She didn't frame them neatly. She didn't try to make them palatable. She trusted me with their rough edges.

That trust humbled me. It reminded me that closeness is not built through grand gestures but through consistency in moments that offer no reward beyond being there. Anyone can show up when things are easy or exciting. It takes something deeper to remain present when nothing is offered in return.

As time went on, we grew more comfortable acknowledging what we were building. Not in public declarations, but in private acknowledgments. In the way she reached for my hand without thinking. In the way, I instinctively moved closer to her in crowded spaces. In the way our conversations stretched beyond the present and brushed gently against the future, not as a fixed destination, but as a shared curiosity.

We talked about where we wanted to go, both literally and figuratively. About careers, aspirations, and the kind of lives we hoped to lead. We did not pretend our paths were identical. There were differences, some practical, some philosophical. Rather than seeing them as obstacles, we treated them as realities to be understood.

That approach did not erase uncertainty. It reframed it.

Instead of asking, "Will this work?" we began asking, "How do we navigate what comes next together?" The difference was subtle yet profound. One question seeks assurance. The other seeks partnership.

There were moments when fear resurfaced, uninvited and persistent. I worried about whether I could provide stability, whether my circumstances would eventually feel burdensome, and whether consistency would one day be mistaken for limitation. These fears did not disappear simply because she cared for me.

But she never confirmed them.

She never made me feel as if I were falling short of some unspoken standard. She measured me not by what I could offer materially, but by how I showed up, my effort, honesty, and willingness to grow. In her eyes, I was not a work in progress in need of correction. I was a person in motion, deserving of patience.

That recognition was transformative. It quieted the internal narrative that told me I needed to earn affection through performance. It allowed me to exist as I was, not as a version of myself striving for approval.

One night, much later, as we sat together in comfortable silence, she asked me what scared me most about caring for someone. The question was gentle, but it reached deep. I thought about it longer than I expected.

"Losing myself," I said finally. "Or realizing I never really believed I was enough to begin with."

She didn't respond immediately. She didn't contradict me or rush to reassure me. She simply took my hand and held it, steady, grounding, present.

"You're not disappearing," she said eventually. "You're becoming visible."

The truth of that stayed with me. By then, love no longer felt like something happening to me. It felt like something I was participating in, actively, deliberately, imperfectly. It was not a state of being swept away. It was a practice. One that asked for attention, humility, and choice.

And perhaps most surprisingly, it did not feel fragile.

What we had built was not dependent on constant affirmation or dramatic reassurance. It was reinforced through reliability. Through showing up again and again. Through choosing honesty over comfort, listening over defense, and patience over certainty.

I began to understand that this was what maturity in connection looked like, not the absence of fear, but the refusal to let fear dictate distance.

As the season shifted and the campus changed with

it, our relationship continued to deepen, not through acceleration but through steadiness. We did not rush toward milestones. We let them emerge organically, trusting that what was meant to take shape would do so in its own time.

Looking back now, I see that this chapter of our story was not about arrival. It was about orientation. About learning to stand beside someone without losing balance. About understanding that commitment is not a promise about the future but a posture in the present.

And in that posture, grounded, attentive, open, I found something I had not realized I was searching for.

A way to stay.

CHAPTER SIXTEEN
Shared Uncertainty

What followed did not feel like a test, though in hindsight I can see that it was. Life has a way of introducing strain not as a dramatic rupture, but as a gradual tightening, small pressures accumulating until they ask something honest of what you have built.

As the spring semester edged toward its close, and with it came a familiar reckoning. Decisions that could once be deferred now loomed, demanding attention. Courses ended, but questions did not. What came next? Where did the effort lead? How long could momentum be sustained before it required something more deliberate?

I felt those questions acutely. I had always measured myself by motion, how hard I worked, how persistently I pushed forward. Stillness unsettled me. Reflection felt indulgent. Yet now, with her beside me, the questions were no longer abstract. They brushed against real possibilities and consequences. They asked not only what I wanted but also how my wanting affected someone else.

She sensed the shift before I named it. She always did.

"You've been quieter," she said one evening as we walked slowly across campus. The air still warm from the heat of the day, carrying the first signs spring was ending.

"I'm thinking," I replied.

She smiled, neither teasing nor concerned. "I know."

That was one of the ways she cared, by recognizing patterns without interrogating them and by allowing space without mistaking it for distance.

Eventually, though, thinking demanded voice.

We sat together on a bench outside the library, its lights glowing warmly against the darkening sky. Students passed in clusters, their laughter trailing behind them, yet we remained anchored where we were.

"I don't know what comes next," I said finally. The admission felt heavier when spoken aloud. "I've always just... kept going forward. But now it feels like the path splits in ways I can't ignore."

She didn't rush to respond. She never did when it mattered.

"What scares you about that?" she asked.

I considered the question carefully. "That choosing one direction means failing at another. If I pause too long, I'll lose momentum. That I'll disappoint people, maybe even myself."

She nodded slowly. "And me?"

The question was gentle, but it reached straight through my defenses.

"I don't want to build something at the expense of you," I said. "Or expect you to wait while I figure myself out."

She turned toward me then, fully. "I'm not waiting," she said. "I'm walking alongside you. There's a difference."

Her clarity steadied me.

What followed was not a resolution but a reframing. We talked, not to decide everything, but to understand where we stood. She shared her uncertainties, the quiet anxieties she carried about timing, ambition, and balance. It became clear neither of us had a finished map. What we had instead was alignment, not perfect overlap, but a shared willingness to adjust.

That conversation marked a subtle shift. It was the first time we explicitly acknowledged that our individual futures were no longer entirely separate. Not fused, not constrained, but connected.

After that, we became more deliberate without becoming rigid. We spoke more openly about priorities. We learned to ask for support without leaning too heavily and to offer encouragement without overstepping. It wasn't seamless. Sometimes we misjudged. Sometimes we stepped on each other's rhythms. But we corrected gently.

There were days when the weight of expectation pressed harder than usual. When fatigue wore thin on patience. When fear resurfaced, persistent and insistent. On those days, love did not feel poetic. It felt practical. It showed u as reminders to eat, as quiet companionship, and as the willingness to sit with discomfort without trying to reframe it.

I learned then that partnership is not about constant harmony. It is about repair. About returning to each other after missteps. About choosing curiosity over assumptions.

One evening stands out with particular clarity. I had received news that unsettled me, nothing catastrophic, but enough to shake my sense of progress. I withdrew instinctively, retreating into silence. When she noticed, she didn't press. She waited.

Later, when I finally spoke, my words came tangled with frustration and self-doubt. I expected reassurance. What I received instead was understanding.

"That sounds heavy," she said.

No minimization. No premature optimism. Just acknowledgment.

It was enough.

That night, I realized something essential: she did not love a version of me untouched by struggle. She loved me within it. That distinction mattered more than I could articulate at the time.

I grew more confident in the understanding that we could maintain both closeness and independence without sacrificing either. This commitment didn't demand constant proximity. Instead, that trust grew as we allowed each other space to breathe.

We now had a steady sense of stability, not complacent or stagnant, but firmly grounded. We stopped questioning the foundation and shifted our attention to how to grow upward while maintaining balance.

Looking back, I see that this chapter was not about achieving certainty but about shared uncertainty. About learning that not knowing does not have to be isolating. That partnership is less about synchronized answers and more about synchronized effort.

Love, I was learning, is not a refuge from complexity. It is a way to meet it with greater courage. And in that courage, something deeper took hold, not loud or dramatic, but enduring.

We were not arriving anywhere yet.

But we were moving forward. Together.

CHAPTER SEVENTEEN
Love Clarified

There came a season when forward motion slowed, not because anything was wrong, but because life demanded a different pace. The urgency that had once driven me began to give way to something quieter, more deliberate. It was unfamiliar territory. I had spent years believing progress could be measured by speed, visible advancement, and the ability to point to something concrete and say, I am further than I was before. Now, progress asks to be recognized in elusive ways.

This shift did not announce itself. It unfolded gradually, disguised as routine.

Days filled with responsibilities that felt ordinary on their own yet collectively demanded everything. Papers were written. Exams were taken. Conversations circled the same concerns without resolution. Life moved forward, but without the dramatic markers I had once relied on to reassure myself that I was advancing.

Through it all, she remained constant, not as an anchor holding me in place, but as a presence that reminded me that movement did not always have to look the same.

That steadiness changed me more than I realized at first.

I found myself less reactive, less consumed by the need to prove something, to myself or to anyone else. I began to consider who I was when I wasn't striving. What remained when ambition loosened its grip.

But survival remained a concern. The fear of poverty had always been one of my driving forces. It had shaped my discipline, my urgency, and my refusal to slow down. And so the question lingered: If I eased my pace, what would happen to everything I was trying to escape?

The answer surprised me.

I was still driven. Still thoughtful. Still deeply invested in my future. But I was also gentler, with my expectations, with my pace, with my own imperfections. Being with her did not diminish my resolve. It refined it.

She had her own seasons of questioning, moments when her confidence wavered beneath layers of responsibility. I learned to recognize those moments not as crises, but as signals, times when listening mattered more than responding, when support meant standing nearby rather than stepping in.

We talked often about balance, how to pursue our goals without losing ourselves, how to remain connected without becoming dependent. These conversations were not theoretical. They were grounded in the realities we navigated daily.

I often reminded her that I was the poorest foreign student on campus and that my life had always been marked by struggle. I carried the weight of being undermined and of having been dealt a difficult hand. I heard relatives' voices in my mind: *"He will return home. He will not amount to anything. America will show him how harsh life is, and he will come back with nothing, without support."* Those thoughts played over and over in my head, and I was determined to prove them all wrong.

That history made me cautious about love, because those were close family members who were supposed to love me. It made it difficult for me to fully trust or depend on anyone. I became resistant. It made me wary of finding a reason to stay, when everything in me had been trained to endure, to survive, and to keep moving forward alone.

I faced challenging experiences both at Dillard, where fellow students often made hostile remarks like "go back to your country" or accused me of being here to steal American education, and women during disagreements. At work, discrimination felt ingrained in company policy. Despite these hardships, my determination to succeed kept me focused. I preferred not to involve others in my struggles, aware of how tough the journey might be. We also had genuine cultural differences; in many respects, we came from completely different backgrounds.

And yet, we learned.

Sometimes we disagreed. Not sharply, not destructively,

but honestly. Differences in perspective surfaced, shaped by our histories and instincts. Where I leaned toward persistence, she leaned toward discernment. Where I pushed forward, she paused to consider. Neither approach was superior. Together, they created something more sustainable.

I began to understand that love does not erase difference. It makes room for it.

One evening, after a long day that had left us both drained, we walked without a destination. The campus was quiet, the sky heavy with clouds that threatened rain but never delivered. Our conversation drifted, touching lightly on everything and nothing.

"I used to think certainty was the goal," I said suddenly. "Like if I could just be sure enough, everything else would fall into place."

She looked at me, curious. "And now?"

"And now I think certainty is overrated," I said. "It can keep you from listening."

She smiled. "I think uncertainty keeps you honest."

That stayed with me.

There was honesty in admitting we did not have everything figured out. In acknowledging that the future was still taking shape, influenced by choices not yet made, that honesty strengthened our connection rather than weakening it. It kept us attentive. Present.

As time passed, our relationship shifted from discovery to cultivation. The initial excitement had not faded; it had transformed, settling into something deeper, steadier, and more enduring. We no longer measured ourselves against possibility. We were living within it.

There were moments when fear resurfaced, when I wondered whether steadiness would one day feel insufficient or whether what we cherished might be mistaken for stagnation. Those thoughts arrived uninvited, shaped by old narratives I had internalized long before her.

But she never rushed me through them.

Instead, she asked questions that invited reflection rather than defensiveness. She challenged me, not aggressively, but thoughtfully. She reminded me that growth did not always require upheaval. Sometimes it required trust.

Trust was becoming a language we spoke fluently.

Not blind trust. Not passive trust. But trust rooted in observation, in consistency, and in the repeated evidence that we showed up for each other, even when it was inconvenient or required patience.

One night, as we sat together in the library, reviewing notes for an upcoming algebra exam, she reached across the table and rested her hand over mine. The gesture was familiar by then, unremarkable on the surface, yet it carried a quiet reassurance that felt almost ceremonial.

"We're doing okay," she said, as if responding to a thought I hadn't voiced.

I nodded, struck by how true it felt.

We were not exempt from struggle. We were not insulated from doubt. But we were steady. And I was learning that steadiness is not the absence of movement;

it is the ability to move without losing orientation.

As the spring term drew to a close, I reflected on how far we had come, not in milestones, but in understanding. I no longer measured progress solely by distance traveled. I measured it by alignment, by how my life felt more coherent and integrated, with her in it.

Love had not simplified my world.

It had clarified it.

And in that clarity, I felt something I had rarely allowed myself before.

Contentment, not complacency, but quiet confidence. The sense that I did not need to rush ahead to prove anything. That where I was, and who I was with, mattered.

We were still becoming, still learning, and still unfolding.

But now, we were doing it with intention.

And that, I understood, was its own kind of arrival.

CHAPTER EIGHTEEN
Becoming Ready

There is a season in every journey when movement is gentle yet essential, when progress cannot be measured by visible change but by inner alignment. It was in this season that I began to understand readiness, not as anticipation, but as preparation. I was no longer waiting for something to happen; I was becoming someone capable of meeting it when it did.

My days settled into a pattern that was demanding but grounding. Mornings began early, often before the sun had fully risen, with the quiet resolve to make the most of each hour. I commuted between work and school with a discipline that left little room for indulgence. Every choice was measured, every expense scrutinized. I learned to live leanly, not out of deprivation, but out of intention. Each sacrifice carried purpose, and that purpose steadied me.

The library remained my refuge. It was there that I felt most aligned with who I was becoming, focused, deliberate, and quietly ambitious. Surrounded by books and muted concentration, I felt a sense of belonging that no physical space had ever fully offered me before. Knowledge, I realized, was not just a means to an end; it was a companion. It gave structure to my days and confidence to my aspirations. With each concept mastered, I felt myself inch closer to the life I was working toward, even if its full shape remained undefined.

Besides, growth is rarely confined to one dimension. While my academic life sharpened my mind, solitude sharpened my self-awareness. Living off campus meant long stretches of time alone that could not be filled with distraction if I hoped to remain steady. In that quiet, I confronted questions I had long avoided. Who was I becoming, beyond survival? What kind of life did I want to build, and what kind of person did that life require me to be?

I came to see that independence is not merely the ability to stand alone, but the discipline to remain grounded without constant affirmation. There were days when fatigue pressed heavily against my resolve, when balancing responsibilities felt overwhelming. On those days, I reminded myself that endurance is often quiet. It does not announce itself with triumph; it reveals itself in persistence.

Deborah crossed my mind occasionally, still without urgency. She remained part of my internal narrative, not as a distraction, but as a point of reflection. Our distance had taught me something valuable: that genuine connection does not depend on constant proximity. What mattered was not how often we spoke or saw each other, but what remained when we did not. The thought comforted me more than I expected.

I began to notice certain shifts in myself. I listened more carefully to others, to circumstances, to my own instincts. I reacted less impulsively, choosing instead to pause, to consider. This was not caution born of fear, but discernment earned through experience. I had learned that rushing rarely produces clarity, and that patience, though demanding, often reveals the truest path forward.

As the semester advanced, challenges continued to surface, unexpected expenses, demanding deadlines, moments of doubt, but none felt insurmountable. I had learned how to steady myself amid uncertainty. I trusted my ability to adapt, to recover, to continue. That trust was new, and it changed everything.

One evening, after a particularly long day, I sat alone in my apartment, the quiet settling around me like a familiar companion. I reflected on the journey so far, the risks taken, the sacrifices made, and the resilience discovered. For the first time, I felt something akin to gratitude for the difficulties themselves. They had shaped me, disciplined me, and prepared me. Without them, I might have arrived at opportunity unformed, unable to sustain what I hoped to claim.

It occurred to me then that readiness is not passive. It is active, intentional, and often invisible. It is forged in moments when no one is watching, when choices are made without applause. It is built through consistency rather than intensity, through commitment rather than impulse.

I did not know what the next chapter of my life would bring. I did not know when or how paths would cross again, or what form connection might take in the future. But I knew something else, with a quiet certainty that surprised me: I was no longer afraid of what was ahead. I had learned how to move forward without certainty, how to trust the unfolding without demanding immediate answers.

If destiny moved quietly, as I had come to believe, then readiness was its counterpart, profound and deliberate. It was the state of being open without grasping, prepared without forcing, grounded without rigidity.

And so, I continued, studying, working, and growing aware that something meaningful does not always announce its arrival. Sometimes it waits until you are ready to receive it.

One afternoon, as I sat absorbed in my studies at the library, surrounded by the familiar hush of turning pages and quiet concentration, I heard a voice behind me, one I recognized instantly.

"Hello, Mark," she said.

I turned, and there was Deborah, standing with an easy smile that felt both unexpected and familiar.

"Hi, Deborah," I replied, momentarily pulling from my notes.

She tilted her head slightly, her tone light but intentional. "So," she said, "when are you going to take me for a ride in your car?"

Her question caught me off guard in the best way. I paused, then smiled. "Well," I said, closing my book slowly, "I suppose I can take a break now."

Carefully, almost reluctantly, I gathered my things and shut my books, marking my place as if to remind myself I would return. We walked out of the library together, our footsteps echoing softly in the hallway before giving way to the open air outside. My car was parked near the front of the lot, waiting in the afternoon light.

We climbed in, and as I started the engine, the sense of formality that had once existed between us faded. We drove along Lake Pontchartrain with the windows cracked just enough to let the water-scented air slip in, the lake stretching beside us like a held breath. The road curved gently, bordered by pale sky and quiet waves, and for a while, there was nothing to do but follow it forward. Sunlight scattered across the surface of the water, and the city felt distant, as if it had loosened its grip. It was one of those in-between moments, unannounced, unremarkable, and yet somehow steadying, where motion itself felt like a form of rest.

The ride was short and unhurried, but it carried more weight than the distance we covered. We talked easily, filling the car with conversation about classes, work, and the small changes in our lives since we had last spent time together.

Laughter slipped in where silence once lingered, and the moments we had missed seemed to fold back into place, as though no time had passed at all. By the time we returned, the drive had become more than just a ride; it was a quiet reconnection, effortless and sincere, reminding me how naturally some bonds resume, even after distance.

During the drive, our conversation drifted naturally toward spending more intentional time together. Before I fully realized it, we had decided to go on a date, our first official one.

CHAPTER NINETEEN
Our First Date

I felt a flicker of uncertainty as I considered where to take her. It wasn't the dramatic kind, the sort that announces itself loudly or demands immediate resolution, but the softer, more private kind that lives in the pauses between decisions. The kind that asks practical questions wrapped in emotional ones. How much could I afford? What would she expect? Would simplicity be mistaken for a lack of effort?

My options were limited, and so were my finances. I was still learning how to balance ambition with reality, how to stretch what little I had while holding on to a sense of dignity. In my pocket was just enough to cover something modest, nothing extravagant, nothing that would announce intention through expense. And for a moment, I considered trying to make it appear like more, choosing a place just beyond my means, hoping confidence might fill the gap where money fell short.

But something in me resisted that instinct.

After a brief pause, I chose honesty.

I told her plainly that I had little. I said it without apology, without embellishment. I suggested something simple: stopping by a Chinese restaurant near campus, then catching a movie afterward. I did not try to dress it up or soften it with excuses. I simply laid the truth between us and waited.

There was a small, almost imperceptible moment of silence, a breath suspended in the air, where I braced myself for disappointment, or at least polite hesitation. But it never came.

She smiled. "Okay," she said.

Just that. No pause. No questions. No polite reframing. Just easy acceptance, offered as naturally as if I had suggested something far grander.

That single word did something unexpected to me. It settled something profound inside my chest, something I hadn't realized was unsettled until that moment. There was no judgment in her response, no hint of expectation beyond the time itself. It felt as though she was choosing the moment with me rather than the place, choosing presence over presentation. And that realization carried more weight than any elaborate plan ever could have.

As we drove, I found myself glancing at her occasionally, watching the way she looked out the window, relaxed and unbothered, as though the simplicity of the evening fit her just fine. I wondered how many people would have dismissed the idea outright;

how many would have masked their disappointment behind politeness. Her ease felt rare. Earned. Almost intentional.

We pulled into the parking lot of the Chinese food restaurant, the kind of place defined more by familiarity than charm. The parking lot was half full, the building glowing with fluorescent light that made everything look slightly unreal, as if suspended outside of time. The smell of fried rice greeted us before we even opened the door, warm, salty, comforting in a way that bypassed sophistication and went straight to memory.

Inside, the restaurant hummed with ordinary life. Families clustered around tables, couples leaned close in quiet conversation, and a group of students laughed loudly in a corner booth. There was nothing remarkable about the setting, and yet, standing there beside her, it felt like the most natural place in the world to be.

We stood shoulder to shoulder studying the menu, smiling at how uncomplicated the choices were. No long deliberations, no careful calculations. Just a shared acknowledgment that sometimes less really is enough. We laughed quietly about it, about how the decision itself felt easier than we had expected.

When we sat down with our trays, the conversation flowed effortlessly. There was no sense of trying to impress, no carefully curated stories meant to elevate ourselves in the other's eyes. We talked about school, classes that frustrated us, professors who surprised us, and the pressure of deadlines that never stopped coming. About work and balancing responsibility with fatigue, about learning to show up even when motivation was thin.

We discussed the tiny details of our days, things people often overlook because they seem too mundane to mention. The paths I used to get to campus. The spots where we studied most effectively. The times that made us laugh when no one else was around. Surprisingly, these small details seemed more revealing than any big revelation.

Every now and then, our laughter drew curious glances from nearby tables. But neither of us seemed to notice, or if we did, we didn't care. There was a gentle rhythm between us, an ease that made time feel less urgent. I became aware, almost suddenly, that I wasn't performing. I wasn't measuring my words or rehearsing responses in my head. I was simply there.

And she was, too.

When we finished eating, neither of us rushed to leave. We lingered for a moment longer than necessary, as if both aware that the night was still unfolding and unwilling to hurry it along. Eventually, we gathered our things and stepped back outside, the heat and steamy contrast to the coolness we were leaving behind.

On the walk to the car, we ran into one of my friends, Ngozi. He asked where we were headed, and I said we were going to the movies. When he asked if he could tag along, I agreed without thinking. Just like that, the two of us became three, and he ended up joining us at the theater.

The drive to the movie theater was calm. The sun was beginning to set, casting long shadows across the road and painting the sky in muted shades of gold and blue. The world seemed to soften at that hour, as though the day itself was exhaling. There was a calmness between us that felt earned rather than forced, a silence that didn't ask to be filled.

Inside the theater, the lights were dim and the air cool. We chose our seats and settled in, the low murmur of other voices fading as the previews began. When the screen lit up, its glow illuminated the quiet closeness we now shared. Our arms rested near each other, not touching, yet aware. It felt intimate without being deliberate, comfortable without being careless.

Words became unnecessary.

Or at least, they should have.

As the movie unfolded, I found myself doing something I have always done, sometimes without realizing it. I leaned in and whispered my thoughts into her ear, small observations about a scene, a comment on a moment that caught my attention, a quiet reaction I did not want to keep to myself. It was instinctive, almost reflexive, born from a desire to share rather than distract.

She did not pull away. She didn't ask me to stop. She listened, occasionally smiling, occasionally nodding, as though my commentary was simply another layer of the experience rather than an interruption. Still, as the movie went on, a familiar doubt crept in. I wondered if I was talking too much, fracturing her immersion, if my need to share was overshadowing her own experience.

Deborah later told me that my friend Ngozi had been leaning over, whispering his own observations about the movie scenes into her ear. In hindsight, the whole situation was comical, and I'm still surprised she wasn't offended that I had agreed to let him tag along. If she was bothered at all, she never let it show. Instead, she laughed about it, and even now, years later, it remains one of those moments she still finds amusing.

By the time the credits rolled, that worry had grown louder. I sat there in the dim light, second-guessing myself, wondering if I had ruined something without realizing it. But even then, even in that moment of self-doubt, the simple act of sitting beside her felt like reassurance enough.

There was something grounding about the shared darkness, the shared light of the screen fading into credits. Something about having occupied the same space, the same stretch of time, without pretense or performance. It felt like confirmation, quiet and undeniable.

When the movie ended, and the theater lights slowly came back on, it was clear that the evening had become more than just a date. It hadn't been marked by dramatic gestures or carefully planned moments. There were no declarations, no turning points that demanded naming. And yet, something had shifted.

It was a beginning, not loud or extravagant, but sincere and honest. The kind that doesn't announce itself, but lingers, waiting to be recognized in retrospect.

As I drove her back to her dorm, the campus passing by in familiar shapes and shadows, I thought about the night as a whole. I thought about how easily it had unfolded, how little effort it had taken to be simply present. And it struck me that what made the evening memorable was not where we went or what we did, but how effortlessly we allowed ourselves to be exactly who we were.

There had been no pressure to impress, no need to pretend. Just two people sharing time, choosing honesty over appearance, presence over performance. In its simplicity, the evening revealed something important, something I would carry with me long after that night faded into memory. That meaningful connections do not require excess. They do not ask for grand gestures or perfect circumstances. They ask only for presence. And that night, quietly and without ceremony, we had given each other exactly that.

CHAPTER TWENTY
A Door Quietly Opened

The days after that evening felt different. Nothing dramatic changed on the surface, classes continued, assignments piled up, routines held, but something had shifted beneath it all. I found myself replaying small moments from that night without meaning to: the way she smiled when she said "okay," the ease of our conversation over greasy trays, the shared silence in the car. These memories did not arrive loudly; they surfaced silently, often when I was least prepared, like a familiar song drifting through an open window.

We did not immediately define anything. There was no conversation about what the night meant or where it placed us. And somehow, that felt right. It allowed the experience to remain unpressured, free to breathe on its own terms. We simply continued seeing each other, crossing paths on campus, sitting together in class, exchanging glances that carried a little more recognition than before.

There was comfort in that unspoken understanding. It felt as though we had crossed a threshold together without needing to announce it.

I began to notice her in ways beyond mere attraction. The way she listened, not just politely, but with genuine attention. The way she paused before responding, as if she wanted to choose words that mattered. The quiet steadiness she carried, even when she laughed. She had a presence that did not demand space yet naturally occupied it.

Our conversations deepened gradually, without force. We talked more about where we came from, about family expectations and personal ambitions. She spoke about her upbringing with honesty, neither romanticizing nor diminishing it. I shared pieces of myself I had grown accustomed to keeping contained, the pressures I felt, the uncertainty I lived with, and the weight of trying to build something meaningful from limited means.

What surprised me most was how safe it felt to speak freely. Not because she always agreed or offered reassurance, but because she listened without judgment. There was no rush to fix or correct, no need to reshape my experiences into something more impressive. She accepted them as they were. And in that acceptance, I felt seen in a way I hadn't anticipated.

Our time together remained simple. Walks across campus stretched longer than planned. Study sessions turned into conversations that wandered far from textbooks. Meals were still modest, unremarkable by any external standard, but increasingly rich in familiarity. We learned each other's rhythms, the times of day we were most talkative, the moments when silence was welcome, the gentle cues that signaled fatigue or reflection.

There were still doubts, of course. I questioned whether I was enough, whether my circumstances would eventually feel limiting to her. Old insecurities did not vanish simply because a connection appeared. But something about the way she moved through the world, grounded, unpretentious, quieted those fears. She never made me feel lacking. If anything, she made me feel more present in my own life.

One evening, days later, as we sat outside watching the campus lights flicker on, she mentioned the movie night again. She laughed, shaking her head, reminding me how my friend had whispered commentary into her other ear.

"I didn't know whether to laugh or focus on the screen," she said, smiling.

I apologized again, half-serious, half-embarrassed.

She waved it away. "It was funny," she said. "Honestly, it told me a lot about you."

I asked what she meant.

She paused, then said, "That you are open with people. That you don't hide who you are." The simplicity of that observation stayed with me. I had always assumed my openness was a flaw, something excessive, something that needed restraint. Hearing it reframed as something meaningful shifted my understanding of myself.

As days turned into weeks, what we were became clearer without ever being formally declared. We showed up for each other in small ways. Sitting together in shared exhaustion, saying very little, needing nothing more.

There was no grand moment when I realized I cared deeply for her. It revealed itself instead through accumulation, through consistency and trust built gently over time. Love, I was learning, didn't require urgency. It asked for patience, presence, and honesty, repeated again and again. However, Destiny was no longer silent.

For a long time, it moved softly through my life, almost politely. It communicated through coincidences that I could overlook, through timing that seemed accidental rather than intentional, and through moments that only appeared significant in retrospect. I had grown accustomed to living alongside it without directly recognizing it. I relied on effort, planning, and endurance, believing that destiny was invoked when outcomes couldn't be explained.

But now, it was insistent. It did not announce itself with spectacle or urgency. It neither demanded action nor offered guarantees. Instead, it pressed forward with clarity, repeating the same truth until it could no longer be dismissed. Something had formed between Deborah and I that was no longer tentative. No longer provisional. It had weight. Direction. And it wanted to be recognized.

What surprised me most was not the depth of the connection but the ease with which it had arrived there.

We never had a defining conversation. There was no

formal request, no moment where I asked her to be my girlfriend and waited for an answer that would change everything. That ritual, so common, so expected, never presented itself naturally. Not because of avoidance, but because it felt unnecessary. The language of our relationship had evolved beyond ceremony. We were already living the answer.

Belonging had settled between us. It revealed itself through patterns rather than declarations. Through the way our days curved toward one another without conscious effort, through the instinctive assumption that the other would be there, not out of obligation, but out of choice. We did not ask for exclusivity from each other. We simply practiced it.

There was no negotiation. We belonged to each other because neither of us wanted to belong anywhere else. I noticed it first in small, almost forgettable moments. When something good happened, I wanted to tell her, not because I needed affirmation, but because sharing it with her felt complete. When exhaustion settled in, she was the presence that steadied me, not by fixing anything, but by reminding me I did not need to carry everything alone.

And I knew I was that for her, too. She did not say it outright. She did not need to. I saw it in the way she spoke my name, casually yet with intention. In the way she referred to the future without clarifying whether I was included, because inclusion had already been assumed. In the way, she adjusted her plans not to accommodate me but to align with us.

We were no longer living parallel lives that

occasionally intersected. We were moving together.

There was a moment, unremarkable by any external standard, when the realization settled fully. We were sitting across from each other, sharing a meal neither of us had planned carefully. The conversation drifted easily, touching nothing urgent. At some point, I realized I felt no need to impress her. No need to manage perception or maintain momentum. I was simply present.

And so was she. That presence carried commitment without naming it. I had spent much of my life believing that commitment required articulation, that without clearly defined terms, relationships would drift into ambiguity. But this was not ambiguous. It was precise in a different way. It was lived rather than spoken. Demonstrated rather than promised.

We had chosen each other repeatedly without announcing the choice. That repetition mattered more than any single declaration could have.

Destiny, in this sense, was not an external force imposing itself upon us. It was the natural consequence of alignment, of values that met without friction, of effort that did not feel extracted, of care that did not require performance. It emerged because neither of us was trying to control the outcome.

We were listening. And destiny, having waited patiently, finally spoke loudly enough to be heard.

There were still uncertainties, of course. Geography had not disappeared. Responsibilities had not loosened their grip. The future remained undefined. But the fear that uncertainty once carried had changed shape. It no longer felt like a threat. It felt like openness.

I did not worry about whether we were "official." We were accountable to each other in ways that surpassed labels. If one of us was absent, it was noticed, not with suspicion, but with concern. If one of us struggled, the other did not retreat. We had learned to stay engaged without intruding, to offer support without erasing autonomy. Love does not always begin with intensity; sometimes it begins with recognition.

Recognition that the person in front of you is not a passing presence. That their absence would alter the shape of your days. That their well-being matters to you not because of what they provide, but because of who they are.

At some point, without marking the day or the hour, we became official. Not in the way people expect. There was no announcement. No social confirmation. No formal transition. We simply stopped considering alternatives. The question of "what are we?" dissolved as the answer became clear in our behavior. We were choosing each other. Every day.

What struck me most was how natural that choice felt. Not effortless, relationships still require work, but unforced. There was no sense of sacrifice in belonging to her, no feeling of narrowing my life. If anything, I felt more expansive, more grounded, more myself.

She did not demand pieces of me I was not ready to give. She accepted what I offered and trusted that the rest would come in time. That trust reshaped how I saw myself.

I had long believed I needed to become more stable, accomplished, and certain before I could be thoroughly chosen. But here was someone choosing me not after the transformation but during it. Not when I had arrived but while I was still building. And she was doing the same.

Our relationship did not hinge on perfection or completion. It thrived in the process. In mutual allowance. In the shared understanding that growth does not invalidate connection, it deepens it.

Destiny, once distant and abstract, had become intimate.

It was no longer something that happened to me.

It was something I participated in.

Looking back, I can see how many moments led us here, how each decision, each restraint, each honest exchange cleared space for this outcome. But at the time, it did not feel orchestrated. It felt alive.

That is how I know it was real, not because it followed a recognizable script, but because it did not need one.

We did not become official because we agreed on the terms. We became official because neither of us was looking elsewhere.

Because we had already learned how to stay. And destiny, no longer content with whispers, had finally spoken clearly enough for both of us to hear. Not as a command but as confirmation.

CHAPTER TWENTY-ONE
The Shape of Commitment

Commitment did not arrive as a declaration. It arrived as a rhythm. It showed in how my days began to organize around a shared awareness, an internal calibration that accounted for her presence even when she was not physically nearby. I noticed it first in the mornings, before the noise of obligation filled the room. I would wake and register the day ahead not only in terms of tasks and deadlines but also in relation to her schedule, her pressures, and her probable fatigue. This was not strategy. It was instinct. A quiet orientation toward another life running alongside mine.

Being "official" did not change the external structure of our lives. Classes still demanded attention. Work still consumed hours. The city remained indifferent to our small victories and private negotiations. But something internal had shifted. The effort I invested no longer felt solitary. Even when we were apart, there was a sense of shared momentum, as though our separate movements were moving in the same direction.

I did not tell anyone immediately. Not because I was hiding it, but because it felt too settled to need explanation. Announcements belong to beginnings that need reinforcement. This did not. It had already proven itself through repetition, through consistency that required no witnesses.

Deborah was the same way. She did not mark the change with ceremony. She simply lived into it. I noticed how naturally she referred to "us" without emphasis, and how plans were framed with quiet inclusion rather than tentative suggestion. She did not check whether I was ready for that language. She trusted I already was.

That trust carried weight.

In the past, commitment had felt like exchanging freedom for security. Now it felt like focus. I was not giving something up; I was giving it shape. The energy I had once scattered across possibilities now gathered with intention. I was still ambitious, still driven, but the direction of that drive had softened. It had become more humane.

We learned from each other in this new context, not as potential, but as chosen. That distinction mattered. Potential invites projection. Choice requires acceptance.

I saw her more clearly once there was no longer a question of whether we were moving forward together. Her habits stood out, not as irritations or idealized quirks, but as patterns I needed to understand. The way she withdrew when overwhelmed. The precision with which she articulated boundaries. The discipline beneath her warmth. Loving her did not mean misunderstanding her less; it meant understanding her more accurately.

She noticed my own patterns, too, how I defaulted to endurance, how I postponed rest until exhaustion decided for me, how I carried responsibility like proof of worth. She did not challenge these traits directly. She asked questions that reframed them. That approach reached me more deeply than correction ever could.

There were moments of friction, not conflict, but adjustment.

Schedules clashed. Expectations emerged unexpectedly. Fatigue eroded patience. We gradually learned to manage tension before it became fixed, to identify discomfort without blame, and to retreat when pride urged escalation. These skills did not come naturally; they were developed through practice.

One evening, after a particularly long week, we sat together in silence longer than usual. I could feel the weight of unspoken things pressing between us, not accusations, but needs waiting to be acknowledged.

"I don't want to disappear into work," I said finally. "But I don't always know how to stop."

She considered that before responding. "I don't want to compete with what matters to you," she said. "I just want to know I still do."

That exchange changed something fundamental. It clarified that commitment was not about prioritizing one thing over another. It was about refusing to let importance become exclusionary. We were not rivals in each other's ambitions. We were witnesses.

Time passed differently after that.

Weeks no longer blurred together. Each one carried its own feel, its own balance of effort and recovery. We became intentional about the spaces we shared. Meals were not always elaborate, but they were deliberate. Walks were not always long, but they were attentive. Even brief check-ins carried weight when offered with sincerity.

Trust had replaced vigilance.

I no longer viewed consistency as reassurance; instead, I trusted the established pattern. When disruptions occurred, I didn't assume they meant anything. I simply asked, and she responded with the same openness she always had.

Our conversations expanded in variety, increasing their scope rather than their intensity. We spoke about our families, not as anecdotes, but as histories that shaped us. We discussed money with candor, ambition with humility, uncertainty without apology. These were not romantic topics. They were necessary ones. They built infrastructure beneath emotion.

I realized then how often relationships fail not because of a lack of feeling, but because of a lack of structure. Affection without scaffolding collapses underweight. What we were building had both.

There were moments when I felt the urge to formalize things, to name milestones, to articulate timelines. That instinct was familiar. It came from a desire for security, not distrust. But each time it surfaced, I examined it more carefully.

Was I seeking clarity, or control?

The answer mattered.

I learned to sit with questions without demanding immediate resolution. To allow the future to remain open without feeling endangered by that openness. Deborah modeled this with ease. She did not rush outcomes. She moved deliberately, trusting that direction revealed itself through engagement rather than speculation.

Watching her do that taught me patience of a different kind.

Not waiting.

Attending.

As spring was coming to an end, the city shifted subtly. The air grew warmer. The streets filled with sound. Life pressed outward. We responded not by accelerating but by grounding. There was something about the season's energy that invited reflection rather than urgency.

One afternoon, we discussed where we were emotionally, mentally, and structurally when we met.

"I wasn't looking for this," she admitted. "I was trying to realign my life."

"So was I," I said.

We sat with that shared recognition. Love had not distracted us from our paths. It had clarified them. It had not interrupted our growth. It had accompanied it.

That realization dismantled one of my oldest assumptions, that a meaningful connection required sacrificing the self. I had believed that choosing someone meant diminishing independence. But what I felt now was reinforcement. I was more myself in her presence, not less.

There were still hard days. Days when work drained me beyond intention. Days when her academic pressures left little room for conversation. Days when the weight of responsibility pressed harder than optimism could counterbalance. But those days did not unravel us. They revealed us.

How we responded mattered more than how we felt. We learned to ask for space without retreat. To offer support without smothering. To apologize without defensiveness. These were not dramatic achievements. They were daily practices. Over time, they accumulated into trust that felt earned rather than assumed.

One night, as we sat together reviewing our respective workloads, I realized something profound: I was no longer performing resilience. I was living it, not as a spectacle, but as sustainability.

That shift changed how I viewed my future. I no longer imagined success as a solitary arrival. I imagined it as shared stability: two people capable of standing on their own, choosing interdependence without fear. That vision felt less heroic than the one I had once held, but far more realistic. And far more appealing.

Deborah never asked me to promise permanence. She did not seek guarantees. She trusted consistency more than declarations. That trust invited my best self forward, not because I feared losing her, but because I respected what we were building.

I understood then that destiny had not forced this outcome. It had responded to readiness.

Readiness to listen.

Readiness to adapt.

Readiness to choose without coercion.

We did not belong to each other because we were afraid of being alone. We belonged to each other because being together made us better able to face what lay ahead.

As the semester drew to a close, pressure mounted. Exams loomed. Deadlines converged. Fatigue returned in familiar waves. But this time, it did not isolate me. I had learned how to ask for help without framing it as weakness. How to receive care without diminishing autonomy.

She did the same.

There was reciprocity in that exchange, not transactional, but balanced. We noticed that the other was giving more than was sustainable. We intervened gently. Not to correct. To preserve.

One evening, after a period of intense activity, we casually strolled without a specific destination. The city hummed around us. Our talk meandered. Eventually, she reached for my hand, not out of need or possession, simply to connect. That simple gesture embodied everything we had discovered: no demands, no fears, just being present.

I thought then about how far I had come, not geographically but internally. How the man I was now would have seemed unrecognizable to the one who first arrived in this city, carrying ambition like armor. That man had believed survival required isolation. He had believed love would compromise focus. He had been wrong. Focus had sharpened through connection. Endurance had softened into sustainability. Ambition had matured into purpose. And commitment, real commitment, had revealed itself not as a binding contract but as an evolving agreement renewed daily through action.

By the time the term neared its end, I felt something unfamiliar.

Confidence without rigidity.

I did not know what the next year would bring. I did not pretend to. But I trusted my capacity to meet it, with discipline, yes, but also with openness. With effort, but also with care.

With Deborah beside me, not as certainty, but as a companion.

That felt like enough.

Not because destiny had promised outcomes.

But because I had learned how to listen when it spoke.

And this time, it spoke not of inevitability, but of choice.

CHAPTER TWENTY-TWO
When Direction Changes

The following day arrived quietly. Morning light seeped into my room as it always did—gentle, impartial, unaffected by any inner changes happening inside. There was no sign of importance in the atmosphere. The city continued its normal rhythm. Buses were delayed. Coffee went cold before being finished. People went about their urgent matters unseen by others, passing by without stopping or noticing each other.

And yet, something had already begun to rearrange itself.

Deborah told me later that afternoon. There was no buildup, no rehearsed gravity in her tone. We sat together in a familiar place, one of those spaces that had absorbed so many conversations it no longer felt like a place so much as a habit. The kind of place where words could land without an echo.

"My program isn't delivering what I expected," she said.

She paused, not for effect but for precision. Deborah had always spoken that way, carefully, deliberately, as if she respected language too much to rush it.

"I've thought about it for a while," she continued. "It's not challenging me the way I hoped. It doesn't align with where I'm headed."

Then, without softening the conclusion, she said, "I'm transferring to another university."

I remember noticing how calm she was as she said it. Not detached. Not uncertain. Just settled. The decision had already been lived with long enough to lose its sharpness.

I didn't interrupt. Some moments ask not to be filled but to be held.

As she spoke, I felt something shift, not suddenly, not violently, but unmistakably. Like a current shifting beneath still water. The facts registered first, cleanly, before emotion caught up. Transfer. Another university. A different campus. A reconfiguration of routines that had grown quietly essential.

But there was no panic.

That surprised me.

Earlier versions of myself might have reacted differently, searched her face for hesitation, rushed to ask what this meant for us, and tried to secure the future before it slipped beyond reach. But none of that surfaced.

Instead, there was space.

I asked questions, but not the urgent ones. I asked what she had learned from the program, what she was looking for now, and what kind of environment she felt she needed. I listened not for reassurance but for clarity.

She spoke of misalignment. Of effort spent without return. Of realizing that patience, while valuable, was not the same as endurance for its own sake. She had given the program time, she said. Enough time to know the difference between temporary discomfort and structural limitation.

"It's not failure," she said, as if anticipating an unspoken assumption. "It's correction."

That word stayed with me.

Correction.

Not escape. Not retreat. Not dissatisfaction sharpened into resentment. Just a measured adjustment, an acknowledgment that direction matters as much as effort.

I recognized myself in that impulse.

There was a time when I would have stayed anywhere that demanded I prove myself. Leaving would have felt like surrender. But I had learned, slowly, that persistence is only meaningful when it serves a purpose. Otherwise, it becomes self-erasure disguised as discipline.

When she finished speaking, I nodded.

"That makes sense," I said.

She looked at me carefully then, not searching for approval, but gauging my response. There was relief in her expression, but also attentiveness. This mattered to her. Not just the decision, but how it would be received.

We did not immediately discuss logistics. We did not discuss distance, schedules, or contingency plans. We let the decision stand without rushing to manage its implications. That restraint felt intentional. Respectful.

Later, when we walked together across campus, the place felt subtly altered, not because it had changed, but because we were now aware of its impermanence. The paths we had taken without thought now felt temporary. The buildings felt less like fixtures and more like chapters.

I noticed how carefully we moved through that awareness. There was no urgency to memorialize anything, no desperation to mark moments as "lasts." We walked at the same pace and spoke with the same ease. Yet there was a heightened attentiveness, a recognition that presence mattered precisely because it was not guaranteed.

That night, after we parted, I sat alone longer than usual. Not because I was unsettled, but because I wanted to understand what I was feeling before naming it.

There was uncertainty, yes. Any honest future contains it. But it was not fear-driven. It did not feel like a threat. It felt like complexity, an invitation to engage more thoughtfully rather than reactively.

I realized then how much I had changed.

Distance no longer frightened me. I had crossed oceans and rebuilt my life from fragments more than once. Geography had never been the real obstacle. What unsettled me was unpredictability, the inability to control outcomes.

But control was no longer my reflex.

I trusted the process now. Trusted presence. Trusted that clarity earned through honesty was more reliable than certainty demanded by force.

Over the days that followed, the reality of her transfer gradually settled in, not as a loss, but as an adjustment. We spoke openly, not obsessively. We acknowledged that things would change without insisting they would deteriorate. We allowed complexity to exist without dramatizing it. There were moments when the difference surfaced unexpectedly. A reference to a class she would no longer attend. A schedule that would soon stop overlapping. These moments landed softly, not as wounds, but as reminders.

I observed another important aspect: she didn't apologize for her choice. That was significant. She didn't present it as something she owed me an explanation for, apart from honesty. She trusted that I could accept her growth without seeing it as abandonment. That trust didn't happen by chance; it was established over time.

And I honored it by not asking her to carry my uncertainty.

We spoke one evening about timing, how rarely it aligns cleanly with connection. Life does not pause its demands simply because two people find each other.

"I didn't plan this," she said. "But I don't regret it."

"Neither do I," I replied.

And I meant both parts of that statement.

Moving forward, work stretched on, and responsibilities multiplied. But something about how I carried them had changed. The weight was still there, but it no longer pressed inward. I was not bracing myself against loss. I was participating in change.

Deborah noticed.

"You're quieter," she said one afternoon. Not

accusing. Observing.

"More settled," I corrected.

She smiled. "That's what it feels like."

Her transfer became real not through paperwork or deadlines, but through conversation. The way she spoke of her future grew clearer as her voice lacked hesitation. Watching that resolve unfold deepened my respect for her, not because certainty is impressive, but because discernment is rare.

I did not feel left behind.

That realization mattered.

Her decision did not diminish me. It did not diminish what we were. If anything, it sharpened the distinction between attachment and alignment. We were not holding each other in place. We chose to stay connected as we moved forward.

That choice required more than feeling.

It required restraint.

There were questions I did not ask, not because I feared the answers but because they were not yet necessary. There were fears I acknowledged privately, without handing them to her for reassurance. That, too, was a form of care.

One night, after a long day for both of us, we sat together in silence. Not the heavy kind. The earned kind.

"This doesn't scare me," she said eventually.

"Me neither," I replied.

And again, it was true.

What I felt instead was attentiveness. A heightened sense of responsibility, not to outcomes, but to integrity. To show up honestly. To remain present. To let change do its work without resistance.

I thought then about destiny, not as inevitability, but as responsiveness. About how often people mistake intensity for meaning, urgency for depth. What we were experiencing felt quieter than that. But it felt real.

When she eventually left that campus, it would not erase what had been built there. It would test it. And I was learning that testing was not the enemy of connection. Avoidance was. The day she told me about the transfer, nothing fractured.

It clarified. It revealed that what we shared was not dependent on convenience or proximity. It endured because we chose to remain engaged with one another as we changed.

That choice did not promise ease. But it promised honesty. For the first time in my life, honesty felt like enough to build on.

CHAPTER TWENTY-THREE
The Space Between Leaving and Staying

As the semester finally came to an end, the campus settled into a particular stillness, one that always arrives after prolonged effort. The hurried steps, the late-night lights in study halls, and the constant low hum of urgency all began to recede. What remained was quieter, more exposed. A pause. An exhale.

For weeks, everything had been moving toward this moment. Deadlines crossed off calendars. Final exams completed. Shifts worked to exhaustion. The end did not arrive suddenly; it unfolded gradually, like a door closing without a sound.

Deborah was getting ready to go back home to California for the summer holidays.

The truth revealed itself not through loud statements but through subtle hints. Suitcases appearing near her bed, marginal notes about packing, and relaxed talks about flights and layovers during our time together, all these small clues were meaningful, even if none required urgent attention.

We had learned not to dramatize transition.

That restraint was mature, an understanding that meaning does not always announce itself loudly. Sometimes it lives in the way you sit beside someone, aware of what is coming, and in choosing presence anyway.

One evening, as the term settled fully into its ending, she said it clearly.

"I'm going home for the summer," she began, her voice steady. "But I want you to know something."

I looked at her, attentive. Not bracing, just listening.

"I'm going to be transferring to another university here in the city," she said. Then, anticipating assumptions she did not want to leave unaddressed, she added, "I'm not going back to school in California. I'm not leaving town."

She paused, not because she was unsure, but because she wanted her words to land exactly where she placed them.

"I'll be back after the summer holiday."

There was no hesitation in her tone. No conditional phrasing. No softening of intent. It was not a promise offered for reassurance. It was a statement of direction.

Something settled in me as she spoke.

Not relief exactly, though there was some of that. Not certainty, but clarity. The kind that doesn't eliminate questions, but reframes them. The kind that doesn't demand response, but invites trust.

I nodded.

"Okay," I said.

It was a simple word, but it carried weight. Not indifference. Not detachment. Acceptance. Alignment.

She studied my face, not anxiously, but carefully, as if confirming something she already sensed.

"I didn't want you wondering," she said.

"I wasn't," I replied honestly. "But I'm glad you told me."

We did not immediately discuss what the summer would look like. We did not map out calls, visits, or timelines. That conversation would come later, naturally, when it was needed. For now, what mattered was the mutual understanding that neither of us was disappearing.

She was leaving temporarily.

She was staying intentionally.

That distinction mattered more than geography.

The days that followed were gentle in a way I hadn't expected. There was no countdown, no pressure to make moments extraordinary. We continued as we had, studying, walking, sharing meals, and sitting in silence when words felt unnecessary. But beneath it all was a quiet attentiveness, an awareness that presence had weight precisely because it was finite.

I noticed how differently I experienced this departure compared to earlier seasons of my life.

Once, separation had felt like a threat. Like something to be endured rather than understood. I would cling to certainty, demand reassurance, and try to stabilize what could not be frozen in place.

Now, I allowed space. Not because I cared less, but because I trusted more.

Trust had become something different to me. It was no longer about guarantees or outcomes. It was about believing that honesty would endure, even across distance. That integrity would not dissolve in the absence. That connection, when rooted in choice rather than proximity, could adapt.

Deborah embodied that.

She did not perform sadness to prove her significance. She did not overstate her feelings to compensate for the distance. She remained herself, present, thoughtful, grounded. And that steadiness made the coming separation feel manageable, even meaningful.

One afternoon, as we walked across campus, we passed places that had quietly shaped us. The library steps where conversations lingered longer than planned. The shaded paths where silence felt companionable rather than empty. The benches where we spoke honestly without needing resolution.

None of it demanded ceremony.

We did not name these as landmarks. We simply moved through them, aware without being sentimental.

"I'll miss this," she said at one point, not pointing to anything in particular.

"I know," I replied.

And that was enough.

As her departure drew closer, my schedule intensified. I had committed to working long hours through the summer, determined to prepare financially for the coming semester. There was little romance in that resolve, just necessity, shaped by discipline. I would stay in New Orleans while she returned home. Different rhythms. Different responsibilities.

But not different intentions.

We talked about that, too, about the imbalance of circumstances and the equality of commitment. About how care does not require symmetry to remain sincere.

"You'll be exhausted," she said one evening.

"I'll manage," I replied.

She smiled. "I know you will. Just don't disappear into it."

"I won't," I said, realizing I meant more than staying in touch. I suggested staying present in my own life and not resorting to isolation as a sign of strength. Not mistaking endurance for disconnection.

That was a lesson I had learned slowly, and she had reinforced it without instruction.

The day she left arrived.

There were no dramatic goodbyes. No public displays. Just a shared understanding carried between us as we stood together one last time before the summer intervened. Her suitcase rested nearby. The future waited, undefined but not intimidating.

"This isn't an ending," she said.

"No," I agreed. "It's a pause."

She nodded. "Exactly."

We embraced, not tightly, not desperately. Just fully. Present. Unrushed.

As I watched her go, I did not feel hollow.

I felt steady.

The city resumed its rhythm around me. Workdays blurred into long evenings. Heat settled heavily into the streets. I moved through my responsibilities with focus, sometimes with fatigue, always with intention.

Beneath everything was the quiet realization that something essential had been created, not lost to distance, or worn down by time. She would come back. Not out of obligation, but because she had decided to. That distinction was significant.

As the summer unfolded, I carried that clarity with me. Not as assurance against difficulty, but as orientation. I knew where I stood and what I was moving toward. For the first time in a long while, I did not feel compelled to rush ahead of the moment I was in.

Destiny, as always, does not announce itself with certainty.

Sometimes, it simply says:

I'm not leaving.

I'll be back.

CHAPTER TWENTY-FOUR
Heat, Labor and the Discipline of Staying

Summer in New Orleans arrived without fanfare. One day the air was merely warm, and the next it pressed against the skin with intent, thick and unrelenting. The city did not ease into the season, it claimed it. Sound traveled differently in the heat. So did time.

With the semester over, my life narrowed to a simpler geometry: work, rest, repetition. I had committed to long hours, not out of martyrdom, but out of necessity. Tuition waited on no one, and ambition, once awakened, rarely slept easily. Each morning, I rose early, not because I wanted to but because discipline had become a kind of faith, something practiced even when motivation wavered.

The campus, once crowded with urgency, now felt hollowed out. Buildings stood open and quiet, their echoes longer, their shadows sharper. I passed places that still held the residue of shared moments, but I did not linger. Nostalgia, I had learned, could soften resolve if indulged too freely.

Work occupied my days, bringing a sense of physical honesty. The fatigue was not driven by anxiety but by effort, leaving my muscles sore and my mind feeling dull. Evenings felt heavy, making sleep more appealing than contemplation. In that weariness, an unexpected clarity emerged: my thoughts became simpler. With no energy left to dramatize loss, I learned to accept it plainly.

I missed her, but not in a way that unseated me. Instead, she appeared in my awareness gently. In the pauses between tasks. In the brief stillness before sleep. In moments when I noticed myself instinctively adjusting plans, as if she were nearby. The connection had not gone dormant; it had gone quiet, like something living beneath the surface.

We maintained regular contact, though not excessive. We exchanged letters and made calls, not to show closeness but as check-ins. Some calls were brief, others more detailed. We didn't try to fill every silence out of duty; instead, we honored each other's natural rhythms. That mutual respect was important.

I noticed how different this summer felt without her being present. There was no frantic need to prove progress. No comparisons to where others were or what they were doing. I was exactly where I needed to be, doing exactly what was required of me. The work was not glamorous, but it was honest.

Some evenings, after particularly long shifts, I would drive through the city as dusk settled. The heat would finally loosen its grip, replaced by a humid softness that invited reflection. In those moments, I felt the shape of my life more clearly, not as a series of sacrifices but as a sequence of choices.

Staying was among my choices. I stayed not due to ease, but because it felt right. I was investing in not just the next semester but also in the person I was becoming, someone able to shoulder responsibilities without resentment and to undertake effort without feeling isolated.

There were days when fatigue tested that resolve. When loneliness crept in quietly, disguised as tiredness, I did not reach for distraction. I rested. I acknowledged the weight without assigning it meaning.

Distance, however, does not weaken a connection if both people continue living honestly. It clarifies it. As summer progressed, I felt something solidifying, not certainty about outcomes but confidence in the process. I was not suspended; I was waiting for her return as proof of direction. My life was moving steadily and deliberately. And somewhere across the country, I trusted hers was too.

CHAPTER TWENTY-FIVE
Returning Without Reverting

California greeted Deborah with a familiarity that did not surprise yet still carried weight. The roads knew her. The light fell differently there, brighter, more forgiving. Even the air seemed to breathe easier.

Home, however, was not a return to who she had been. It was a place to recalibrate. Family filled the early days; questions were asked with affection, and expectations were wrapped in concern. She answered honestly but selectively. She was not hiding anything. She simply no longer felt the need to explain herself fully to be understood.

She noticed how much she had changed. Her routines felt looser now, less dictated by urgency and more by intention. She woke earlier than she needed to, read more than she used to, and started her summer job at Sears. Her work schedule was tight, with only occasional time for friends and relaxation.

Thoughts of the upcoming transfer came often, but without anxiety. She had already made the decision. The remaining uncertainty was logistical, not existential. For the first time in a long while, her future felt responsive rather than imposed.

She told me she thought of me often, not with longing that pulled her back but with steadiness that anchored her forward. She said I was part of her life now, not as an interruption but as context. Someone who knew her trajectory and did not try to redirect it. That mattered more than she had expected.

There were moments when old patterns tempted her, comforts that belonged to earlier versions of herself. But she recognized them quickly. She had outgrown certain rhythms. Certain compromises. Growth, she realized, is not loud. It simply refuses to go backward.

Our conversations demonstrated this. When we talked, it was about sharing experiences, not filling a void. I didn't expect her to miss me as a show, nor did she reassure me out of duty. There was a trusting bond that didn't need constant affirmation to stay strong. She carried that trust with her as summer unfolded.

Some afternoons were spent outdoors, contemplating how different this season was from previous ones. She had thought that distance would seem like a break, but instead, it became a reminder that what they shared was not entirely reliant on being close. She was growing into more of herself, not in isolation, but with the comforting awareness that someone saw her clearly and still chose her.

When thoughts turned toward returning to New Orleans, they carried anticipation rather than relief. She was not escaping home. She was moving toward alignment. Toward a life she had chosen deliberately. And toward me, not as a guarantee but as a continuation.

She did not count days.

She trusted time.

Together, these summers did not pull us apart.

They proved something quietly essential:

That staying and leaving can coexist.

That growth does not require abandonment.

That connection, when grounded in choice, survives distance without demanding proof.

CHAPTER TWENTY-SIX
Same City, Different Campuses

As the summer break ended, Deborah returned to New Orleans. The city received her as it always did, without pause, without sentimentality. The heat was thick, persistent, and unapologetic. The air clung to skin and clothing, as if to remind anyone arriving that comfort was never guaranteed here, only continuity. Life did not wait for reunions. It resumed.

Her return did not feel like a reset. It felt like a continuation shaped by absence.

She arrived with the quiet confidence of someone who had already made peace with transition. There were boxes, books, clothes, the artifacts of a temporary home, but there was also resolve. She had not come back to reclaim what had been paused. She had come back to step into something new.

The new school year began almost immediately.

Her transfer was complete. A new university across the city. New buildings with unfamiliar layouts. New professors whose expectations were not yet clear. New classmates who did not know her history or habits. I, in contrast, returned to the same campus I had left in the spring, hallways that recognized me, routines that felt worn in, and a structure I understood well enough to move through without friction.

Same city. Different campuses.

The phrase surfaced early, not as a point of tension but as a description. We said it once, almost offhandedly, and then let it settle. It did not require elaboration. It held both nearness and distance, continuity and divergence. It is named the reality without exaggeration.

Our first meeting after her return was unceremonious. No dramatic reunion. No attempt to compress weeks of separation into a single moment. We met, embraced, and sat down as if conversation had been interrupted rather than suspended. Summer had shaped us, but not in ways that demanded performance. We noticed the changes instinctively, the steadiness in her posture, the softness in my pacing, the way silence felt less urgent than before.

She told me about California in fragments.

About being home without fully belonging there anymore. About family conversations that felt both comforting and constricting. About the clarity that followed distance, the confirmation that returning to New Orleans was not hesitation but intention. She did not dramatize her decision. She spoke of it as alignment rather than escape.

I listened without interrupting. Not because I was holding back, but because her words did not invite correction or commentary. They stood on their own.

My summer was quite uneventful, with long hours, repetitive tasks, and honest fatigue. I shared with her the challenges of my security guard duties and my taxi driving, highlighting the discipline involved. I explained how exhaustion had instilled in me restraint rather than resentment. I didn't present it as a sacrifice, and she didn't view it that way either. There was a mutual understanding in that moment: that effort, when undertaken intentionally, doesn't require romanticization to be deemed worthy of respect.

"You seem grounded," she said at one point.

"So do you," I replied.

And that felt accurate, not flattering.

The semester unfolded quickly.

Her days were filled with orientation sessions, administrative hurdles, and the mental labor of becoming new again. I watched her navigate this with composure, but not without effort. There were evenings when she was quieter than usual, when the weight of adaptation pressed down harder than she admitted. I learned not to mistake that quiet for distance.

I did not try to solve her adjustment.

I asked questions when she invited them. I listened when she spoke. I stayed present without demanding articulation. That restraint was not passive; it was deliberate. It came from understanding that support does not always announce itself.

My own return to Dillard was marked by familiarity.

The same professors. The same expectations. The same academic pressures that had shaped previous semesters. But my relationship to them had changed. Summer had stripped away the urgency I once mistook for motivation. I approached the work with steadier intention. I no longer believed endurance alone proved commitment.

I paced myself.

That choice altered everything.

We settled into new routines gradually.

Gone were the days of accidental encounters between classes or shared study sessions born of convenience. Now, every meeting was deliberate. Planned. Chosen. We compared schedules not out of obligation, but out of respect for each other's time. When an overlap appeared, we protected it carefully.

That intentionality changed the nature of our connection.

Presence became something we offered consciously rather than assumed. And in that offering, it gained weight.

There were early weeks of adjustment that tested us.

She referenced classmates whose names meant nothing to me. I mentioned projects she could not visualize. We learned each other's new rhythms through conversation rather than observation. That shift required patience. Curiosity replaced familiarity, and listening replaced assumption.

We asked questions.

Not to keep score. To stay connected.

One afternoon, I visited Loyola University between classes. She walked me through the buildings as if narrating her days aloud helped anchor them. I watched her explain the decisions she had made about her course load, her reasoning confident and unmistakable.

"I think this was the right move," she said, not seeking validation but stating a conclusion.

"I believe you," I replied.

That belief was not rooted in optimism. It came from observation. From watching her tolerate discomfort without dramatizing it. From seeing her choose alignment over familiarity. I was learning that growth often appears as consistency rather than spectacle.

Our relationship reflected that truth.

We were not accelerating.

We were stabilizing.

There was no urgency to set a landmark, no anxiety about where this was headed. We spoke about the future when it came up naturally, not to seek reassurance, but as an extension of shared awareness. The city gave us just enough distance to practice autonomy without drifting apart.

Different pressures. Different victories. Different failures. But a shared orientation.

There were days when we did not see each other at all. Weeks when deadlines crowded out spontaneity. Messages shortened. Calls shifted to later hours. But absence no longer triggered panic. We had learned to distinguish between unavailability and withdrawal.

That distinction mattered more than proximity ever had.

One evening, after a particularly long day for both of

us, we met to go for a walk in Audubon Park. No destination. No agenda. The city hummed around us, cars passing, voices overlapping, life continuing, indifferent to our private conversation.

"You don't seem like you're bracing anymore," she said quietly.

"I'm not," I answered. "I don't feel like everything is fragile."

She nodded, as though confirming something she had already noticed.

Trust, as I have learnt, does not require constant reinforcement. It required consistency.

As the semester gained momentum, responsibilities layered on top of one another. Exams loomed, projects accumulated. Fatigue returned in familiar waves, but it no longer isolated me. I had learned to ask for support without interpreting it as failure, to rest without apologizing for it, and to keep moving forward without losing myself in the process. Deborah mirrored that balance.

She did not vanish into her new environment, nor did she cling to familiarity. She adapted with intention. Watching her do that deepened my respect, not because adaptation is impressive, but because it is honest.

There was no single moment when I realized this chapter was different.

No defining scene.

Just a series of quiet confirmations.

A shared meal after a long day. A message sent without needing an immediate reply. A disagreement handled without defensiveness. A pause is respected without requiring explanation. These were not milestones. They were foundations.

One night, as we sat together, she was reviewing her notes on various subjects, each with its own goal. I noticed something quietly profound.

We were no longer proving anything.

Not our commitment.

Not our resilience.

Not our worthiness.

We were simply showing up wherever we could, with what we had.

That realization shifted how I understood success.

I no longer imagined it as a solitary arrival. I imagined it as shared stability: two people capable of standing on their own, choosing interdependence without fear. That vision felt less heroic than the one I had once held, but far more sustainable.

And far more real.

Deborah never asked me to guarantee outcomes.

She trusted consistency more than declarations. That trust invited my best self forward, not because I feared losing her, but because I respected what we were building.

As the weeks passed, I became aware of something else. I was no longer organizing my life around contingency.

I was not waiting to see how things turned out before engaging fully. I was already engaged academically, emotionally, and structurally. Deborah was not a variable I was managing. She was a presence I was integrating.

And I was, in turn, part of her life, not as an anchor that restricted movement, but as a point of reference that offered stability.

Same city. Different campuses.

Different trajectories.

But a shared direction.

One evening, as we sat in my car outside her dorm, Cabra Hall, she paused.

"I don't know exactly what this will look like a year from now," she said.

"I don't either," I replied.

She studied my face briefly, then smiled. "But I'm not afraid."

"Neither am I."

That felt like enough.

As I drove home alone, I thought about how different it felt from certainty. Certainty had always promised safety but demanded control. This, whatever it was, asked only for presence.

And presence, I realized, was something I could provide consistently. Not because situations were stable or results were certain. But because I simply was. For the first time, I wasn't striving to reach a destination. I was already here, same city, different campuses.

And somehow, more aligned than ever. I did not know what the next season would ask of us. I only knew that something had settled into place, not as certainty but as orientation. We were no longer reacting to change; we were moving with it. Whatever came next would not arrive as an interruption but as a continuation. For the first time, I trusted that we would meet it not by holding tighter but by staying present, together yet whole.

CHAPTER TWENTY-SEVEN
Pressure Without Fracture

Momentum did not arrive as acceleration. It arrived as a weight. The weeks that followed carried a different density, less tentative, more demanding. The semester no longer felt new enough to excuse uncertainty, yet not settled sufficiently to offer ease. Expectations tightened. Time compressed. Decisions began to stack instead of spacing themselves politely across the calendar. This was the season when intentions were tested not by crisis, but by accumulation.

I felt it first in my body. Mornings came earlier. Evenings stretched thinner. The margin I had worked to preserve narrowed under the pressure of deadlines, work hours, and the quiet insistence of progress. But something crucial had changed: I no longer saw that pressure as a threat. I understood it as information.

At my campus, the pace quickened. Professors assumed equal readiness and resilience. Assignments were layered, not sequential, demanding sustained attention rather than bursts of effort. I found myself returning to the library with a familiarity that bordered on muscle memory, but my approach was no longer reactive. I worked with structure. I stopped earlier. I left when diminishing returns threatened clarity.

This restraint felt unnatural at first. For years, I had equated commitment with depletion. If I wasn't exhausted, I assumed I hadn't given enough. Now I was learning to trust a different metric, one that valued continuity over spectacle.

Deborah felt the pressure too, though it took a different shape. Her new campus demanded more than coursework. She navigated unfamiliar systems, expectations whose logic had not yet revealed itself, and the subtle exhaustion of being new, all while refusing to shrink. There were days when she spoke with precision and resolve, and others when her words slowed, as if choosing carefully what to say.

I learned to identify those shifts without explicitly naming them. Support, I realized, was not a scripted action; it was a stance.

We did not see each other as often during that stretch. Schedules overlapped less generously. Evenings that once invited lingering now required planning. But what we lost in frequency, we gained in clarity. When we met, we arrived with intention. There was no need to perform presence; it was already implied by the effort it took to create it.

One evening, we met halfway between our campuses, a habit that had become symbolic without trying to be. We walked for a while before speaking, letting the day drain from our systems.

"I feel like everything is asking something of me at once," she said eventually.

"Me too," I replied.

That symmetry brought relief, not because it resolved issues, but because it alleviated isolation. We weren't faced with overwhelming opposition; instead, we were managing parallel pressures.

"I don't want to harden," she added. "I don't want productivity to flatten me."

I understood that fear intimately.

"I don't think you will," I said. "You notice when things start to cost too much."

She considered that, then nodded. "So do you now."

That acknowledgment carried more reassurance than encouragement ever could. We were no longer in the stage of discovering each other. We were at work sustaining what that discovery had made possible. That work was quieter and far less romanticized, but it was real. It showed up in how we negotiated time without resentment, adjusted expectations without keeping score, and trusted absence without inventing meaning.

There were moments of friction, inevitably. One evening, after a tiring day, I canceled plans that I should have called off sooner. She clearly showed her disappointment, and I didn't try to excuse my fatigue. Instead, we sat with our discomfort until we understood it, and then we moved past it.

"I don't need you to push past your limits," she said. "I just need to know when you're reaching them."

That distinction stayed with me. I realized how often conflict is less about opposition than about timing. How many misunderstandings arise not from disagreement but from delayed communication? We were learning to intercept those moments before they hardened into distance.

Pressure reveals patterns. When overwhelmed, I tend to focus narrowly on solving, fixing, and containing. When stretched thin, Deborah tries to grasp the bigger picture of her burden by seeking context. Neither reaction was incorrect, but both needed translations.

Realizing that translation was a different kind of progress, I experienced a sudden change halfway through the semester. I noticed that decisions, small and unremarkable, were increasingly made with a shared awareness baked in. Not consultation, not permission, but consideration. If I stayed late on campus, I checked in. If she anticipated a demanding week, she named it early. These gestures were not negotiations. They were acknowledgments.

We weren't just managing each other; we were keeping tabs on each other. That distinction mattered more than I had expected. There was a night when everything felt especially heavy. I had worked late, studied longer than planned, and still felt behind. When we met, I was quieter than usual, my attention fractured by unfinished tasks.

She noticed.

"Do you want company," she asked, "or do you want

quiet?"

The question disarmed me.

"Company," I said after a moment. "But quiet company."

She nodded, as if that made perfect sense.

We sat together without speaking, the city moving around us, neither demanding nor distracting. In that silence, I felt something stabilize. Not because anything had been resolved, but because nothing needed defending.

I thought then about how rare that kind of understanding is... not intuitive, not assumed, but earned through attentiveness.

As the semester pressed on, success began to look different to me.

It was no longer defined by completion alone but by preservation, of health, of clarity, of connection. I was learning that progress that consumes its own foundation eventually collapses. What we were building required a different pace.

Deborah seemed to be arriving at a similar conclusion.

She spoke one afternoon about taking on fewer commitments and resisting the impulse to prove herself through overload. "I want my effort to mean something," she said. "Not just look like something."

I smiled. "That sounds familiar."

We laughed, not because it was ironic, but because it was shared.

By then, I understood that momentum does not always feel fast. Sometimes it feels heavy because it is carrying something worth protecting.

Pressure did not fracture us. It clarified us.

We were learning how to stay responsive without becoming reactive, how to remain ambitious without becoming brittle, and how to choose each other not as an escape from difficulty but as a context for facing it.

There were still unknowns ahead, structural, practical, and inevitable. We did not pretend otherwise. But the fear that once accompanied uncertainty had softened into something else: respect.

Respect for the work ahead.

Respect for the people we were becoming.

Respect for the fact that some things cannot be rushed without being damaged.

As the term approached its midpoint, I felt a quiet assurance, not that everything would work out, but that we would not disappear under the weight of trying. We were learning to hold pressure without losing shape. And that felt like the beginning of something more substantial than certainty.

CHAPTER TWENTY-EIGHT
Drawn Closer

The story did not slow down because we were busy. If anything, it deepened.

School consumed us in different ways that semester. The demands were no longer theoretical or introductory, they were precise, relentless, and unforgiving of distraction. Deborah carried the weight of a new academic environment, learning not only the material but also the culture, rhythm, and expectations. I brought something more layered: coursework that required sustained focus, paired with the practical necessity of survival. Tuition deadlines did not take intellectual curiosity into account. Rent did not pause for exams. Responsibility, once fully assumed, does not negotiate.

I worked longer hours than ever before, juggling shifts as a security guard at Bayou State Security and filling the gaps by driving for Yellow Cab.

Early mornings bled into long days. Evenings slipped into shifts that ended when the city was already quiet. My body learned new definitions of tired, fatigue that settled into the bones, exhaustion that didn't announce itself loudly but waited patiently for stillness. There were nights when I returned home knowing I had just enough energy to prepare for the next day and nothing more.

And yet, strangely, I did not feel defeated.

Pressure had become familiar terrain. What unsettled me was not the weight itself but the precision required to carry it without letting anything essential slip. Every hour mattered. Every choice had consequences. I quickly learned that discipline was not about intensity, it was about sustainability.

Deborah understood that instinctively.

She never questioned why my availability shifted or why my schedule tightened. She saw the structure forming around me and did not try to break it open. Instead, she adjusted to it, not shrinking, not demanding, simply adapting with awareness. That generosity was not loud. It was steady.

We saw each other less often, but when we did, the time felt magnified.

Sometimes it was only an hour, a quiet meal squeezed between obligations, a walk cut short by commitments waiting on either end. But those moments carried a different charge now. We were no longer lingering in possibility. We chose each other despite the constraints.

That choice mattered.

There were evenings when I arrived exhausted, my mind still calculating hours and expenses, deadlines and balances. Deborah would look at me carefully, as if reading my unspoken thoughts.

"You don't have to be on right now," she'd say.

And something in me would soften.

We learned to be together without needing to perform. Some nights were light, filled with laughter and relief. Others were quiet, marked by presence rather than conversation. We learned to recognize when the other needed grounding rather than distraction.

Destiny no longer waited politely in the background.

It intervened in ordinary ways.

An accidental scheduling overlap gave us an unexpected afternoon together. A shift change that ended early on a day she happened to be free. A canceled plan that created space for something better. None of it felt dramatic, yet all of it felt intentional, as if life itself were adjusting small variables just enough to keep us aligned.

The closeness grew not from abundance, but from scarcity.

Time was limited. Energy was rationed. Yet affection intensified. Desire sharpened. We became more deliberate in our touch, in our words, in our attention. When I held her, it felt like an arrival rather than an escape. When she leaned into me, I felt trusted rather than needed.

We were lovers now in a fuller sense, not defined by novelty but by choice under pressure.

One night stands out.

I had worked a double shift, my longest in weeks. My body was spent, my mind dulled by repetition. I considered canceling our plans, convinced I had nothing meaningful to offer. But something urged me forward, not obligation or guilt, just a quiet pull.

When I arrived, she looked at me and smiled, that familiar smile that never asked me to be more than I was.

"You're exhausted," she said.

"I am," I admitted.

"Sit," she replied, already moving closer.

She rested her head against my chest, and for a moment neither of us spoke. The day's noise drained away. My breathing slowed. The tension I hadn't acknowledged finally eased.

"I don't need you at your best," she said softly. "I need you here."

That sentence rewired something in me.

For so long, love had felt conditional on capacity, on performance, availability, and strength. But this was different. This love did not ask me to arrive polished. It asked me to arrive honestly.

And I could do that.

The financial pressure did not disappear. If anything, it intensified. There were weeks when I counted every dollar, calculating margins that left no room for error. I learned the discipline of saying no to convenience, to rest, and sometimes even to desire. Responsibility has a way of clarifying priorities without ceremony.

Deborah never minimized that reality. She didn't romanticize my struggle or turn it into a narrative. She respected it.

Before We Understood

Sometimes she helped practically, packing food for me, adjusting plans to cut costs, and choosing simplicity without making it feel like a compromise. Other times, she helped simply by believing in my capacity to endure without losing myself.

That belief mattered more than relief.

Our conversations shifted during that season. We spoke less about possibility and more about process, less about what we hoped would happen, more about how we were handling what already was. We talked about boundaries, about limits, about how to protect what we were building without isolating it from reality.

That honesty was intimate.

Destiny did not sweep us away from responsibility. It anchored us inside it.

I began to notice how instinctively we moved toward each other, even when exhausted. How disagreement, when it surfaced, no longer threatened us but sharpened understanding. How silence between us felt safe rather than distant.

We no longer questioned if this connection could withstand pressure; instead, we observed it becoming stronger because of it.

There were moments of doubt, of course. Nights when the future loomed too large, when I wondered whether I was asking too much of endurance, time, and her. But each time that question surfaced, something answered it, not with reassurance, but with evidence.

Her presence, my stability, our shared choice: One evening, after a long walk, she paused and looked at me intently.

"You're carrying a lot," she said.

"Am going to be fine," I replied.

She smiled softly and said, not cheerfully, but sincerely, "Good."

That's when I realized that destiny was no longer just something happening around us. It became something we actively participated in. Not passively or romantically, but intentionally. Regardless of exhaustion, pressure, or uncertainty.

We were being drawn closer, not because life had become easier, but because we were learning to stand together in difficulty. And that, I realized, was the most valid form of intimacy we had known so far.

CHAPTER TWENTY-NINE
What We Built In Motion

Nothing about my circumstances improved suddenly. In fact, the pressure intensified. My course load grew more complex, demanding not only time but sustained concentration. Work expanded rather than contracted, with each additional shift less optional than the last. Rent did not negotiate. Tuition did not change. Responsibility did not pause to acknowledge effort. Every obligation arrived on schedule, indifferent to fatigue.

But something fundamental had changed in the way I carried all of it.

The weight was still there, distributed across deadlines, financial strain, and the quiet anxiety of long-term planning, but it no longer rested solely on my shoulders. It wasn't that Deborah took the burden from me. She didn't. What she did instead was more enduring: she became part of the structure that kept me upright under it.

There is a difference between help and balance. I was learning that balance lasts longer.

Our lives during that season did not align neatly. They interlocked. Her academic demands surged in waves, papers, group projects, and exams that demanded total immersion. Mine followed a steadier but relentless rhythm: classes, work shifts, nights stretched thin, and mornings arriving too early. There were weeks when our schedules seemed designed to test us, when the only overlap came in brief phone calls at the edge of sleep or messages exchanged between obligations.

We quickly learned that proximity alone would no longer sustain us.

Closeness had to be intentional.

We stopped relying on chance encounters or routine overlap. Every moment we shared became chosen, planned, and protected. As a result, it carried a different kind of weight. Time together was no longer assumed; it was offered. That offering changed how we showed up.

I began planning my days differently, not to squeeze more in, but to leave something intact. I became more honest about my limits and less inclined to prove endurance for its own sake. Deborah noticed the shift before I named it.

"You don't run yourself into the ground the way you used to," she said once, half-observing, half-affirming.

"I still get tired," I replied.

"Yes," she said, smiling. "But you stop now."

That distinction mattered. I had spent years believing that stopping meant failure. Now I was learning that stopping at the right time was preservation.

Deborah was learning her own version of this lesson. Her transfer had placed her in unfamiliar academic terrain, new expectations, new standards, and a new social landscape that demanded emotional energy to navigate. I watched her absorb the challenge with composure, though not without effort. She never dramatized her fatigue, but I learned to recognize the signs, the quieter evenings, the longer pauses before she spoke, the way her shoulders carried tension when she thought no one was watching.

I chose not to fix those moments but to learn how to meet them. Support, I realized, isn't always about providing answers; it often manifests as steadiness, a simple presence that doesn't ask for anything in return. There were occasions when Deborah had to fully immerse herself in her work to escape everything else.

"I'm going to be scarce for a bit," she told me once, her voice calm yet firm. "I need to focus."

"Take your time," I said without hesitation. "I'll be here."

And I meant it. Not as reassurance or sacrifice, but as trust. Trust that absence did not mean retreat. Trust that focus did not mean abandonment.

That trust changed everything.

When she resurfaced days later, exhausted yet lighter, the reunion felt grounded rather than frantic. We did not rush to make up for lost time. We acknowledged the effort instead. We honored what had been required of her rather than what had been withheld from me.

That established our pattern. Effort was more important than availability. Intent held more weight than immediacy. Of course, the city remained indifferent to everything.

New Orleans moved at its own pace, loud, humid, unapologetic. It asked only that you keep up or step aside. I worked longer shifts that season, sometimes stacking them back-to-back, leaving my body sore and my mind dulled. I learned to conserve energy in ways I never had before, to rest without guilt, to eat without rushing, to recognize the early signs of burnout before they demanded attention.

Fatigue stopped feeling like an enemy.

I treated it as information.

Deborah noticed that too.

"You're different lately," she said one evening as we sat quietly, sharing space more than conversation.

"How?" I asked.

"You're not bracing," she said after a moment. "You're steady."

That word stayed with me.

Steady did not mean easy. It did not mean relaxed or carefree. It meant aligned. It meant I was no longer torn between who I was and who I believed I had to be. Work, study, and love were no longer competing identities. They were integrated into a single life. That integration changed how I loved her.

Affection no longer felt like an escape. Desire no longer felt like relief. Being with Deborah did not pull me away from my responsibilities; it pulled me deeper into them. She did not distract me from the life I was building. Instead, she clarified why I was building it. We became more expressive without becoming dramatic.

Touch grew quieter yet more certain. Words became fewer yet more deliberate. We learned to read the spaces between sentences, to recognize when silence was comfort rather than distance, and when space was restoration rather than retreat.

There was an afternoon that crystallized everything. I had just finished a shift that hollowed me out completely. The kind that drains not only energy but also optimism. I sat in my car longer than necessary, hands resting on the steering wheel, watching the world move without me. For a moment, I considered going straight home, shutting the day down, and retreating into solitude.

Instead, I drove to see her.

She didn't ask questions. She didn't offer solutions. She opened the door, took one look at me, and wrapped her arms around my neck. That was it. No commentary. No fixing. Just contact.

I rested my forehead against hers and exhaled. Slowly. Intentionally. The tension slipped away in increments, not because my problems were solved, but because I no longer held them alone.

At that moment, I realized something vital: love isn't always about reassurance. Sometimes, it manifests as permission to stop pretending to be strong... permission to be held without needing to explain, and permission to rest without feeling guilty.

That was when it became clear that destiny was no

longer pushing us ahead. Instead, it was walking alongside us, neither leading nor pulling, just keeping pace.

We began speaking more openly during that season, not in grand declarations, but in honest fragments. About ambition. About fear. About how to protect each other without stifling growth. We acknowledged uncertainty without dramatizing it. The future remained undefined, yet it no longer felt threatening.

We were learning to coexist with the unknown. Tensions still arose at times. Fatigue tested my patience, and stress made me more reserved. Even so, I sensed a change. Conflict no longer felt like a break but a shift in understanding.

We addressed tension before it hardened. We disagreed without escalating. We apologized without defensiveness. These were not dramatic achievements. They were daily practices.

One night, after a rare disagreement that was resolved not through compromise but through understanding, Deborah said something quietly definitive.

"We don't disappear when things get hard."

She was right.

Neither of us pulled away. Neither of us used distance as punishment. We stayed connected, not because it was simple, but because it was important. That was the shape of what we were building. Not intensity. Not certainty. But continuity.

Over time, I shifted my notion of success from merely enduring to staying present throughout the process. Deborah adopted the same perspective. We were no longer living parallel lives of mere survival; instead, we were weaving them together, carefully and intentionally, without forcing harmony where it wasn't natural.

Destiny had not eliminated obstacles.

It had provided clarity.

And direction, once known, does something remarkable: it quiets fear. Not by removing risk but by anchoring purpose.

Late one evening, as we parted outside her building, she studied my face.

"You're tired," she said.

"Yes," I replied.

"But you're okay," she continued.

"I am," I said.

She smiled, neither seeking reassurance nor offering consolation.

"Me too," she replied.

As I drove away, the streetlights stretched ahead of me, and I realized something I hadn't before. Love was no longer something I fit into my life only when space allowed. It was part of how I moved through it. And that knowledge, earned, tested, and steady, did not feel like an arrival. It felt like momentum.

CHAPTER THIRTY
The Quiet Acceleration

Momentum builds quietly, gathering unseen until you realize you're no longer pushing, you're being carried.

That's how the next season unfolded. Nothing outwardly changed. My schedule stayed packed. Her coursework remained demanding. The city stayed unforgiving. Bills arrived. Deadlines loomed. Fatigue tested me. Yet something unmistakable was happening beneath the surface. We were accelerating. Not toward an outcome but into a deeper version of who we already were.

I noticed it in small ways first. In how my thoughts began to include her without effort. In how decisions are formed with her presence already accounted for, not as a constraint but as a constant. I no longer paused to ask whether making space for her would cost me anything.

The cost-benefit analysis had dissolved. She was not an addition to my life; she was part of its operating system.

That realization did not make life easier. It made it clearer. There were mornings when I woke before dawn, my body heavy with accumulated exhaustion, my mind already cycling through tasks awaiting completion. On those mornings, I did not romanticize discipline. I simply stood and began. Work had stripped ambition of its glamour, leaving behind something more reliable: responsibility embraced without resentment.

Deborah had an instinctive grasp of rhythm. She never demanded explanations for my absences or expected me to dilute my truths for her ease. When my responses were delayed, she didn't see it as avoidance. When my voice sounded strained, she didn't think I was indifferent. Instead, she focused on my intent rather than the tone of my words.

That kind of listening is rare. It also taught me how to listen better.

Her days were layered with pressure. The new university demanded adaptation at a pace that left little room for error. She was learning to assert herself in unfamiliar academic spaces, to claim authority without overexplaining, and to trust her competence without waiting for validation. I watched that confidence assemble itself slowly, not as bravado, but as grounded certainty.

We spoke often about effort.

Not as a complaint.

As context.

"Today felt heavy," she would say.

"I know that feeling," I'd reply.

And sometimes that was all that needed to be said.

A special closeness develops when two individuals cease trying to impress through resilience, instead permitting their efforts to be seen without exaggeration. They trust that simply being acknowledged suffices. That was the space we inhabited.

Our time together grew more substantial. We no longer needed to fill the silence with affirmation. Presence carried its own weight. We worked on different material, occasionally exchanging a glance that said more than any conversation could.

Those moments reshaped my perspective. They made me realize that I don't need to escape my life to feel connected. I can stay fully present in it and still experience fulfillment.

One evening, after another long stretch of back-to-back responsibilities, I found myself doing something unexpected.

I was not seeking rest or relief, but rather continuity. I wasn't counting down to a conclusion; I was looking forward to returning to the rhythm. That was a new experience.

In the past, endurance had always been fueled by the promise of reprieve. Push now, recover later. Survive this, then breathe. But now, breathing was built into the process. Rest was not deferred; it was integrated.

Deborah had taught me that, not through instruction, but through example.

She rested without apology. She protected her focus without guilt. She refused to glorify depletion. Watching her live that way slowly dismantled my belief that worth was proven. There were still moments of tension, inevitable, unavoidable. Stress has a way of testing even the most stable foundations. There were evenings when my patience thinned, and financial pressure pressed harder than optimism could counterbalance. There were days when her workload made her distant despite her best efforts.

However, something important had changed. We no longer saw tension as a danger. Instead, we tackled it promptly, softly, and without drama.

"I'm stretched thin," I would say.

"I know," she'd respond. "What do you need?"

That question alone changed everything.

Sometimes the answer was space. Sometimes reassurance. Sometimes, nothing more than acknowledgment. We learned not to take each other's capacity personally. Capacity fluctuates. Commitment does not.

That distinction gave us freedom.

Destiny, once an abstract idea I had associated with inevitability, began to take on a different meaning. It was no longer about being led toward a predetermined outcome. It was about being shaped by repeated choice.

Choice to stay present.

Choice to adapt.

Choice to remain open even when certainty was unavailable.

One afternoon while walking together through a neighborhood neither of us knew well, Deborah stopped suddenly.

"Do you ever think about how different this could

have been?" she asked.

"All the time," I said.

"And does that scare you?"

"No," I replied after a pause. "It steadies me."

She smiled, as if that answer confirmed something she had already suspected.

What steadied me was not the idea that we were destined to succeed. It was the knowledge that we were capable of responding to change without losing ourselves or each other.

That capability felt earned. We did not rush to define the future. We spoke in outlines rather than details, in possibilities rather than promises. Not because we lacked commitment, but because we respected complexity.

We understood that lives do not unfold in straight lines. They curve, pause, and reroute. We were learning to move with that truth rather than resist it.

Late one night, after a day that had demanded everything, I had to give, I found myself driving home alone, the city quieter than usual. Streetlights reflected off damp pavement. The air was heavy but still.

I thought about the man I had been when I arrived in this city, how tightly I had held control, how suspicious I had been of anything that threatened my focus. I had believed love would scatter me.

I had been wrong.

Love, when chosen deliberately, had concentrated me.

It had given my effort context, my sacrifice meaning, and my discipline direction.

And Deborah, steady, perceptive, unafraid of change,

had become not a destination, but a companion in motion.

When I reached my door, I didn't feel the urge to collapse or retreat. I felt grounded. Capable. Still tired, yes, but not hollow.

The momentum was no longer fragile.

It was sustained.

And for the first time, I understood that the most powerful transformations do not announce themselves through upheaval.

They arrive quietly, and then they stay.

CHAPTER THIRTY-ONE
The Forward Pull

Acceleration, I learned, does not always feel like speed. Sometimes it feels like gravity.

Nothing in our lives announced that things were changing. There were no declarations, no moments set aside for reckoning, no conversations framed as turning points. And yet, day by day, I could feel the distance between us closing, not because we rushed toward each other, but because we stopped resisting what was already happening.

Our relationship had begun to change. With less hesitation. Less internal negotiation. Less need to protect the edges.

We were closer now, not just emotionally, but structurally. Our lives began to lean toward each other in an almost imperceptible way. Schedules adjusted without discussion. Priorities quietly reorganized. Decisions carried an unspoken awareness of "us," even when neither of us named it aloud.

I first noticed it in my thinking.

I no longer imagined my future as a solitary construct she might later be invited into. Instead, when my thoughts drifted forward, to the next semester, the next year, the shape of stability, I saw her there automatically. Not inserted. Not imagined. Simply present.

That realization startled me with its calmness.

There was no urgency attached to it. No pressure to turn it into plans or promises. It existed as orientation, not an agenda. Like a compass settling without instruction.

Deborah was doing the same, I think.

She spoke differently now, not about the future explicitly, but about continuity. About what she was building rather than what she was escaping. About sustainability rather than survival. Her choices reflected a growing confidence that she no longer needed to keep her life provisional.

We were both done living as if everything were temporary. That shift did not make life easier. It made it more honest.

There were evenings when she arrived, tired in a way that had nothing to do with workload and everything to do with adaptation. Being new was draining more energy than she cared to admit. Learning environments. Reading people. Establishing credibility. All of it required vigilance.

She never framed it as a struggle. But I learned to hear the quiet fatigue beneath her composure.

I responded not by fixing but by staying.

That staying, consistent, unadorned, became our language.

We spent more time together, not because we forced it, but because separation now required effort. Seeing each other felt less like an event and more like a default state we returned to whenever circumstances allowed.

Sometimes we worked side by side. Sometimes we ate in comfortable silence. Sometimes we talked late into the night about nothing that sounded important yet felt essential.

Those moments accumulated.

They built something solid beneath us.

I realized one evening, while watching her read across the table from me, that my nervous system no longer braced itself when I thought about the future. There was no tightening, no urge to preemptively protect myself from disappointment.

Instead, there was curiosity.

A calm attentiveness.

I was not asking, *Will this last?* I was asking, *How do we grow without breaking what's working?*

That was new.

With Deborah, forward movement felt like integration.

I was more myself with her, not less.

She did not dilute my ambition. She clarified it. She did not compete with my discipline. She refined it. Being with her did not scatter my focus; it organized it.

She noticed that, too. "You're different lately," she said one afternoon as we sat by the Lakefront.

"How?" I asked.

"Quieter," she said after a moment. "But more certain."

I considered that. "I don't feel like I'm fighting everything anymore."

She nodded. "That's what I see."

We didn't say more. We didn't need to.

The future hovered near our conversations without ever being summoned. We spoke of classes yet to be taken, responsibilities yet to be completed, and possibilities still taking shape. But always with an underlying assumption of continuity.

Not *if.* Just *how*.

That assumption did not feel naive. It felt earned.

It rested on evidence, not hope. On patterns, not promises. On how we showed up, consistently, imperfectly, intentionally.

Our closeness deepened not through intensity but through reliability.

There were no emotional spikes to chase. No uncertainty to prompt reassurance. The connection held its shape even on ordinary days, especially then.

Those were the days that mattered most.

One weekend, after an especially demanding stretch of work and study, we found ourselves sitting together with nothing scheduled and nothing urgent pressing in.

The stillness felt unfamiliar at first.

Then welcome.

We talked about small things. Laughed without

effort. Let time stretch without trying to control it. At some point, she leaned her head against my shoulder, not as a claim, not as a signal. Just because it felt right.

That moment carried more weight than any declaration ever could.

It told me something essential: we were no longer building toward closeness.

We were living inside it.

And with that closeness came an unmistakable forward pull.

I began to notice how naturally my mind moved beyond immediate survival. I still worked hard, calculated expenses carefully, and carried responsibility seriously. But I was no longer operating in emergency mode.

I could imagine stability without feeling reckless.

I could imagine shared outcomes without feeling trapped.

Those thoughts did not require articulation. They existed as a quiet orientation, shaping how I moved through the present.

Deborah mirrored that shift.

She spoke with increasing confidence about her place at her new university, not as a trial period, but as a foundation. She made choices with longer horizons in mind. She invested herself without hedging.

Neither of us said what that meant for *us*.

But neither of us needed to.

The closeness was already doing the work.

There were still moments of friction, misalignment, and fatigue-induced misunderstanding. We did not become immune to stress or human limitations. But we had developed a shared reflex: address rather than avoid, clarify rather than assume, pause rather than escalate.

Those reflexes protected us.

They allowed acceleration without instability.

Late one night, driving her home after a long day, she slipped her hand into mine with quiet certainty. The gesture felt different, not tentative or exploratory. Settled. I realized then that something profound had happened. We were no longer questioning whether we belonged in each other's lives. We were asking how to steward what we had. That question carried responsibility, but not fear. As we reached her building, she stopped and turned toward me.

"You seem... solid," she said softly.

"So do you," I replied.

She smiled, not brightly, but with recognition.

And as I drove away alone, I felt the acceleration again, not rushing, not destabilizing it.

Just a steady pull forward.

Toward a future we were already preparing for, without having to name it yet.

CHAPTER THIRTY-TWO
What Was Already Taking Shape

There comes a moment when effort stops feeling like resistance and begins to feel like acceptance, not resignation, but recognition. That was where I found myself. Nothing had been announced. Nothing had been claimed out loud. And yet, something undeniable had taken hold.

Our lives were full, crowded, demanding, unyielding. My days were stretched thin by coursework and work hours that left little margin for rest. Tuition loomed constantly in my thoughts. Rent, utilities, food, transportation, each obligation pressed forward without concern for timing or fatigue. Some mornings, I woke already tired, my body heavy with the accumulation of days that had asked more than they gave back.

But I was no longer carrying that weight alone.

Before We Understood

What surprised me most was not that our relationship survived the pressure, but how naturally it absorbed it. There was no sense of competition between responsibility and closeness. No quiet resentment. No tally of sacrifices. The person I had to be to endure and the person I was becoming with her no longer felt divided.

Exhaustion still visited me, but it didn't isolate me anymore.

Deborah noticed the strain before I found the words for it. She always did. She didn't interrupt my momentum or try to soften reality. She didn't ask me to slow down when slowing down wasn't possible. Instead, she adjusted her presence with an almost intuitive care.

Sometimes, it was a meal waiting for me after a day of not eating. Sometimes, it was a short message sent just when my resolve weakened. Sometimes, it was simply her sitting nearby while I worked, her presence steady and unobtrusive, reminding me that effort doesn't have to mean disappearing.

That kind of closeness did something profound to me. It didn't weaken my determination. It steadied it.

There were nights when I came home worn down to something quieter than exhaustion, when ambition felt distant and survival the only goal. On those nights, I didn't need reassurance. I needed grounding. And she gave it without my having to ask.

She was carrying her own weight.

A new academic environment demanded constant adaptation. She was proving herself again, among professors who didn't yet know her rigor, classmates who hadn't seen her discipline, and systems that required her to start from scratch. She never dramatized the strain, but I could hear it in the pauses between her words and in the way her shoulders relaxed only after the day was done.

When she spoke of her days, she didn't filter them to protect me or to put on a strong face. She let me see the uncertainty alongside the confidence. That honesty drew me closer than any declaration ever could.

Our spaces began quietly merging.

My apartment stopped feeling like a place I passed through between obligations. It began to feel lived in. Her dorm room became familiar, not because I was there often, but because I felt at ease. We didn't announce arrivals. We didn't keep track of how much time we spent.

We showed up.

The connection no longer required tending.

It breathed on its own.

I noticed a shift in how I thought about the future.

When I imagined the months ahead, another semester, heavier responsibilities, the slow work of building stability, she was there. Not as a plan. Not as an assumption. Just present.

Not an anchor. A direction.

That realization carried unexpected emotion.

I had spent so long believing that love would distract me from my purpose and that closeness would dilute my ambition. Instead, I felt sharper, more honest, and more aligned. The fear that I would have to choose between survival and connection dissolved quietly, without fanfare.

She felt it, too.

I heard it in the way she spoke of her days, of plans still forming, of challenges ahead. There was no defensiveness in her tone. No bracing for loss. Just openness, an ease born of trust built slowly and honored consistently.

We were no longer circling each other.

We were moving forward together, close enough to be affected, separate enough to remain whole.

Some evenings were unremarkable on the surface. We sat together with no agenda. Conversation drifted and returned. Silence lingered without discomfort. Those moments held a depth I hadn't known how to name.

They weren't intense. They were safe.

And that safety moved me more than intensity ever had.

One night, after a stretch of long shifts and restless sleep, I admitted something that had been forming quietly inside me.

"I don't feel like I'm waiting for this to fall apart anymore," I said.

She looked at me, not startled, not relieved. Just attentive. "What do you feel instead?"

I searched for the right word, "Present," I said finally. "Like I'm allowed to be here."

Her eyes softened. "That's how it feels for me, too."

That moment stayed with me, not because it was dramatic, but because it was true.

We weren't clinging.

We weren't testing.

We weren't proving.

We were choosing, again and again, without ceremony.

The future remained unnamed, not avoided but unforced. It was shaping itself through repetition, reliability, and the quiet courage of returning to each other day after day.

I began to understand something I had missed for years.

Destiny does not arrive loudly. It reveals itself through consistency.

What once felt like a coincidence now felt intentional, not imposed, not rushed, but earned. The path ahead wasn't guaranteed, but neither was it fragile.

As responsibilities continued to pile up and days demanded more than comfort allowed, something unfamiliar settled in me.

Not certainty.

Confidence.

Not in outcomes, but in us.

Whatever came next would not interrupt my life. It would grow out of it.

We were already becoming part of the future we hadn't named yet.

CHAPTER THIRTY-THREE
Where Do You See Yourself?

The shift did not arrive suddenly. It announced itself through repetition, through questions that lingered a little longer than before and through pauses that asked for more than reassurance. Deborah did not press. She never had. But she had begun to look forward with a steadiness that invited me to stand beside her and look, too.

I noticed it first in the way she spoke about time.

Not days or weeks, but seasons. The next year. The one after that. She referenced them casually at first, almost experimentally, as if testing how the words felt in the open air. There was no demand in her voice, no expectation hidden behind implication. Just curiosity. Intention. A quiet readiness.

One evening, after dinner, we sat together longer

than usual. The day had been heavy for both of us, lectures, deadlines, responsibilities layered tightly together, but neither of us moved to fill the silence. Outside, the city carried on in its familiar rhythm, indifferent and alive.

She broke the quiet gently.

"Can I ask you something?" she said.

I nodded, already attentive.

"Where do you see yourself… not immediately," she clarified, "but beyond this?"

The question did not feel abrupt. It felt earned.

I leaned back, considering not how to answer, but how honestly I could answer without retreating into abstraction. In the past, I might have deflected, spoken in general terms about goals, or framed ambition without anchoring it to reality. But something about the way she asked made that feel insufficient.

"I see myself stable," I said slowly. "Not just surviving. Building something that doesn't collapse the moment pressure hits."

She watched me carefully, not interrupting.

"I want a future where effort leads somewhere sustainable," I continued. "Where I'm not always bracing for loss. Where work has purpose beyond endurance."

She nodded, absorbing the words. Then she asked the question beneath the question.

"And where do I fit into that picture?"

There it was.

Not an ultimatum.

Not a demand.

An invitation.

I felt the weight of it, not as pressure, but as responsibility. The responsibility to answer clearly, without hiding behind uncertainty or fear of saying too much.

"I don't think of my future without you," I said. The words surprised me with their ease. "Not as a dependency. As a presence. As someone whose life intersects with mine in ways that matter."

Her expression softened, but she didn't look away. She was listening not for comfort, but for truth.

"I'm not asking for guarantees," she said quietly. "I know how unpredictable life is. I just need to know whether you're imagining forward with me, or if you're keeping that door half-closed."

That honesty moved me.

I thought about the man I had been when we met, how guarded he was with hope, how carefully he rationed his expectations. That man believed commitment required certainty, and certainty felt dangerous. But I was no longer that man.

"I'm imagining forward," I said. "I just don't want to rush past what we're building now by naming things before they're ready."

She smiled, not because the answer relieved her, but because it aligned with what she already felt.

"That's fair," she said. "I don't want to rush either. I just needed to know we were facing the same direction."

We sat with that understanding, letting it settle without embellishment. Something was grounding about saying just enough and stopping there.

After that conversation, I became more aware of the

future in subtle ways.

Not as a looming question, but as a presence quietly forming in the background. I noticed how Deborah spoke about her studies now, not just in terms of completion, but also in terms of application and where they might lead. How they might fit into a larger picture. She spoke about work she found meaningful, about impact, and about building a life that reflected intention rather than reaction.

And I listened in a new way, not defensively or cautiously, but attentively.

My own thoughts began to shift in response. I found myself considering logistics I had once avoided, not because I feared them, but because they required me to imagine continuity. I thought about where I might be in a few years, what kind of stability I was working toward, which sacrifices were temporary, and which I no longer wanted to normalize.

These thoughts didn't overwhelm me.

They clarified for me.

There were moments when doubt still surfaced, old fears whispered that planning was premature, and that hope invited disappointment. But those voices no longer controlled the conversation. I acknowledged them and moved forward anyway.

Deborah didn't push when she sensed hesitation. She asked questions instead.

"What matters most to you in the long term?"

"What do you want your life to feel like, not just look like?"

"What are you willing to work for, and what are you

no longer willing to lose yourself over?"

No one had asked me those questions so directly before.

Answering them required more than ambition. It required honesty.

I told her about my fear of instability and how deeply it had shaped my decisions. I told her that financial pressure had taught me discipline, but it had also made me wary of dreaming too freely. I admitted that part of me still measured safety by survival rather than fulfillment.

She didn't argue with that.

She reached for my hand instead.

"I don't need everything figured out," she said. "I just need to know that you're not shutting the future out to protect yourself."

That landed.

I wasn't shutting it out anymore.

I was learning how to hold it carefully.

As weeks passed, the conversation continued, not in one long discussion, but in many small ones. Sometimes in passing. Sometimes late at night, when the world had quieted enough to make space for reflection. Each time, the tone was the same: open, grounded, mutual.

We didn't make declarations.

We made room.

I noticed how naturally we began discussing shared possibilities,

Not as commitments, but as considerations if we lived here longer. If work took us there. If our paths converged in ways we couldn't yet define. None of it felt forced. It felt exploratory.

And that exploration brought a closeness deeper than certainty ever could.

One night, after a long conversation about nothing and everything, Deborah leaned against me and said softly, "I like who you are when you think forward."

That stayed with me.

Because I liked him too.

He was not reckless.

Not rigid.

Not afraid.

He was present, intentional, and open.

And for the first time, imagining the future did not feel like tempting fate.

It felt like acknowledging something already in the making.

We didn't name our destination.

But we stopped pretending we weren't headed anywhere. And that was enough, for now.

CHAPTER THIRTY-FOUR
The Shape of What Was Coming

Following that conversation, nothing seemed outwardly different, but everything felt different. Not necessarily lighter, but more purposeful.

The days continued with their familiar demands. My schedule remained unforgiving: long hours at work, coursework that refused to ease, and obligations that did not pause just because my inner world had shifted. Deborah, too, was immersed in her studies, which still required constant adjustment. On the surface, our lives looked the same as they had weeks earlier. But beneath that surface, something had aligned.

There was a new attentiveness between us, not the fragile kind born of fear of loss, but the grounded kind born of shared awareness. We listened more carefully. We chose our moments more deliberately. Time together was no longer something we fit in; it was something we protected.

I started to realize how seamlessly she had integrated into my inner world. As I organized my week, she was already part of it, not as a burden but as a steady presence. When I thought of feeling relief from exhaustion, I envisioned her being there. In moments of joy or hardship, she was the first person I wanted to share with.

This realization didn't frighten me.

It steadied me.

One evening, after I finished a late shift, I went to see her without announcing myself. I didn't want to talk. I didn't want advice or reassurance. I just wanted proximity. When she opened the door and saw the fatigue etched on my face, she didn't ask questions. She stepped aside and let me in.

We sat together in silence, the kind that doesn't demand to be filled. My head rested against the back of the couch; hers against my shoulder. Outside, the city moved on, unaware of something quiet yet consequential unfolding in that small room.

"You don't have to carry everything alone," she said eventually, not as instruction, but as a reminder.

"I know," I replied. And for the first time, that knowledge felt lived rather than learned.

I told her about the pressure I'd been under, the numbers, the deadlines, the constant calculation required to keep everything balanced. I didn't dramatize it. I didn't minimize it either. I spoke plainly, the way one does when trusting the listener not to panic or judge.

She listened the way she always did: thoroughly.

Not interrupting.

Not fixing.

Just present.

"I believe in what you're building," she said when I finished. "Even when it's still invisible."

Those words mattered more than she knew.

Because much of my life had been spent working toward things no one could yet see. Enduring processes without applause. Trusting that effort would eventually yield something stable. Her belief didn't remove the difficulty, but it gave it context.

As the weeks passed, I noticed another shift.

I was no longer compartmentalizing my life into isolated sections, work here, school there, and a relationship somewhere in between. Instead, these parts began to speak to one another. My decisions at work were shaped by the future I was slowly allowing myself to envision. My approach to school became more strategic and less reactive. Even rest felt purposeful rather than indulgent.

Deborah was part of that integration.

She challenged me without pressure. She asked questions that demanded clarity without imposing her timeline. When I hesitated, she didn't interpret it as withdrawal. When I spoke confidently, she didn't assume permanence. There was a mutual understanding that growth doesn't follow a straight line.

One afternoon, we met between classes and walked without a destination. The air carried that familiar mix of warmth and humidity, making movement feel slower, more deliberate.

"Do you ever think about where this city fits into your life long-term?" she asked.

I considered it carefully.

"I think it's where I'm becoming myself," I said. "I don't know if it's forever. But it's important."

She smiled. "That makes sense. Some places are chapters, not conclusions."

"What about you?" I asked.

"I think I'm still deciding," she said. "But I know I want wherever I end up to feel intentional. Chosen."

We walked on, letting the idea settle.

Neither of us said it, but we were both thinking the same thing: wherever we went, we were starting to imagine not going alone.

That thought didn't demand resolution.

It offered direction.

There were still difficult moments. Nights when exhaustion wore down my patience. Days when stress made me withdraw more than I intended. But the difference now was repair. We addressed tension early, before it calcified into distance. We spoke honestly about our needs without framing them as accusations.

One disagreement, in particular, stood out, not because it was intense, but because of how it ended.

We had misunderstood each other about the plans we'd made. Nothing major. Just enough to frustrate us both. In the past, I might have gone quiet, choosing internal withdrawal over confrontation. This time, I didn't.

"I think we're talking past each other," I said. "Can we reset?"

She looked relieved. "Yes. Please."

We clarified. We listened. We adjusted.

And afterward, instead of feeling drained, I felt closer to her than before.

That was new.

Conflict had not weakened us.

It had refined us.

One night, much later, she asked softly, "Do you realize how much you've changed since we met?"

I thought about it.

"I think I'm less afraid of being seen," I said.

"I see that," she replied. "And I don't take it lightly."

Her words reminded me of something essential: vulnerability was no longer something I offered reluctantly. It had become part of how I loved.

And love, whatever shape it was taking, was no longer abstract.

It lived in the ordinary.

In shared meals after long days.

In messages sent simply to check in.

In the way we reached for each other without ceremony.

We didn't announce that we were moving forward.

We just kept moving.

Together.

As the semester pressed on, momentum built, not only academically or professionally, but emotionally. There was a sense that we were approaching something, not a deadline, not a decision, but a deeper threshold of awareness.

I could feel it.

Not as urgent.

As readiness.

I didn't know exactly what the future would ask of me. I didn't know how many variables were still unresolved. But I knew this: when the moment came to speak more clearly about where I stood, I would not retreat.

Because whatever was forming between us was no longer fragile.

It was becoming real.

And I was no longer afraid to meet it.

CHAPTER THIRTY-FIVE
What Remained When the Year Released Us

As another school year drew toward its close, the city seemed to exhale with us.

The pace shifted suddenly at first, deadlines announced themselves more loudly, syllabi thinned, and conversations grew shorter and more purposeful. Libraries stayed lit later. Everyone moved with the shared awareness that something was ending, even if no one said it out loud.

For me, the pressure intensified before it softened.

Final projects demanded precision. Exams required focus bordering on stubbornness. Work hours stretched as expenses refused to wait politely for academic closure. I moved through my days with discipline, not adrenaline, guided less by panic than by resolve. I had learned over time that urgency burns quickly, but intention sustains.

Deborah was navigating her own version of that

narrowing corridor.

Her first year at Loyola was coming to a close, carrying the weight of the transition she had quietly borne for months. I watched her juggle final papers, presentations, and the emotional accounting that comes with proving, mostly to oneself, that a decision was the right one.

We saw each other less in those final weeks.

Not because we were drifting, but because life demanded our attention elsewhere. When we did connect, it was often late, brief conversations that carried more meaning than length. A shared laugh over exhaustion. A few minutes of quiet presence before sleep. A message sent simply to say, I'm still here. And that was enough.

One evening, after my last exam, I sat alone in my car before driving home. The campus was quieter than usual, as if the buildings themselves were tired. I realized then how much this year had changed me, not in dramatic ways, but in posture, in how I carried responsibility, and in how I allowed myself to be supported.

I didn't feel triumphant.

I felt complete.

A few days later, Deborah and I met after she submitted her final paper. We didn't plan anything elaborate. We walked. We talked. We let the moment be without trying to shape it into something symbolic.

"It feels strange," she said, breaking the silence. "Like I should feel more relieved than I do."

"I know what you mean," I replied. "It's less relief, more... release."

She nodded. "Exactly."

We sat on a bench by the Mississippi River, watching the water flow with unhurried certainty. There was something grounding in that continuity, a reminder that endings don't stop motion. They redirect it.

"This year mattered," she said quietly. "Not just academically."

"I know," I answered.

We didn't list reasons. We didn't recount milestones. We didn't need to. The meaning was already shared.

There was an unspoken awareness between us that summer was approaching, bringing its own questions. Schedules would change. Distance might reappear in new forms. Familiar routines would loosen their hold. The structure that had framed our growth was dissolving.

And yet, neither of us seemed afraid.

"I'm proud of you," she said suddenly.

"For what?" I asked.

"For how you stayed," she replied. "Even when things were heavy. Even when it would have been easier to disappear into work or stress."

Her words landed softly but intensely.

"I stayed because I wanted to," I said. "Not because I had to."

That distinction mattered.

As the school year officially ended, my life didn't suddenly become easier, but it became clearer. The absence of academic deadlines revealed what had been quietly forming beneath them: a steadier sense of self, a relationship built on presence rather than proximity, and a future that no longer felt abstract.

Deborah and I didn't make declarations about what summer would bring.

We simply acknowledged that whatever came next would be navigated the same way this year had been, intentionally, honestly, together.

On the last evening before campus emptied further, we stood outside her place, reluctant but unhurried.

"This doesn't feel like a pause," she said.

"No," I agreed. "It feels like a continuation."

She smiled, and in that moment, I understood something essential: the year had not been a test we had passed or failed. It had been a foundation.

And now, standing at its edge, I wasn't measuring what I might lose.

I was recognizing what I had built.

Whatever the next chapter demanded, I knew this much: I would meet it grounded, not grasping. Present, not provisional.

The year was ending.

But what mattered most was not.

CHAPTER THIRTY-SIX
Between Naming and Becoming

The school year ended the way things often do when their meaning has already settled deep enough that it no longer needs ceremony.

There were no markers that announced it for us, no celebratory dinners, or symbolic closures. Instead, the ending arrived through subtraction. Fewer emails. Fewer obligations. The slow thinning of campus life as students packed cars and boarded planes, carrying their temporary versions of themselves back to wherever summer would place them. The city loosened. Time stretched. The pressure that had governed our days... released.

Deborah left for California a few days after finals.

We moved through those last days with an ease that surprised me. Packing happened without stress.

Conversations drifted between practical details and comfortable silence. There was no frantic attempt to capture everything before the distance returned. We had already learned that urgency did not strengthen us; it only distorted the moment.

When we said goodbye, it was simple.

An embrace that lingered just long enough to say this matters, without clinging. A final look that held more understanding than words ever could. Then she was gone, folded back into her other life, her other coast, her other rhythm.

I stood there longer than necessary after she left.

Not because I was unraveling, but because I was honestly registering the absence. This time, it didn't feel like a test. It felt like a pause, intentional, temporary, purposeful.

The next morning, I went back to work.

And I doubled down.

Longer hours. Extra shifts. Fewer days off. I welcomed the structure because it gave my body something concrete to do while my mind worked through less tangible terrain. Physical fatigue was honest. It asked nothing philosophical of me. You showed up. You did the job. You went home.

Work had always been my refuge.

In the past, it had been a shield, something I used to avoid sitting with uncertainty or feeling for too long. This time, it was different. I wasn't hiding behind it. I was standing inside it, using it as a container rather than an escape.

Days passed in repetition. Heat pressed down

relentlessly. Sweat marked the hours. Paychecks came and disappeared just as quickly into rent, tuition, and utilities, the quiet obligations that don't ask how you're feeling before they demand to be met.

There was dignity in that grind.

But there was also space.

And in that space, my thoughts returned, again and again, to Deborah. Not to her absence exactly, but to the conversation we had just before she left. It replayed not as dialogue but as atmosphere. As a subtle shift in gravity.

She hadn't pushed.

That was what stayed with me.

She had spoken carefully and deliberately, her tone inviting honesty rather than defensiveness. She had wondered aloud, not accused, not demanded. She had asked questions that didn't seek immediate answers, only awareness.

Where do you see this going?

What does the future feel like to you?

Are we moving toward something... or simply moving together?

She hadn't framed it as an ultimatum. She hadn't asked me to decide on the spot. She had simply opened a door and trusted me to walk through it when I was ready.

That trust weighed more than pressure ever could.

Left alone with her questions, I couldn't dismiss them. They followed me through workdays and into quiet nights. They surfaced when my hands were busy, but my mind was free. They waited patiently while I tried to put them off.

What we had was real.

That was no longer in question.

It had endured distance. It had adapted to shifting schedules, different campuses, and uneven availability. It had grown not through intensity or spectacle but through repetition, through choosing each other again and again without announcement.

But was choice without language sufficient?

I had always believed that naming things altered them, that words fixed what was meant to remain fluid and definitions narrowed what could otherwise breathe. Flow had felt safer. Movement without labels allowed growth without expectation.

Or so I told myself.

Now, that belief felt incomplete.

This wasn't fear of commitment masquerading as philosophy. I knew fear well enough to recognize it. This was something else. It was caution born of respect, for her, for myself, and for what we were building.

I didn't want to name something prematurely and risk reducing it to an expectation. But I also didn't want to hide behind ambiguity if clarity was being quietly invited.

The truth revealed itself slowly and without mercy.

I wasn't afraid of losing her.

I was afraid of misnaming what mattered.

Words carry weight. Once spoken, they shape reality, create accountability, and change how others listen, and how we listen to ourselves.

But avoidance carries weight too.

And lately, continuing "with the flow" no longer felt

neutral. It felt like a decision disguised as patience.

One night, after a double shift that left my body aching and my thoughts unusually sharp, I sat alone in my apartment, the lights off. The city hummed outside, cars passing, distant voices, life continuing without regard for my internal deliberations.

I let the question surface entirely for the first time, without softening it.

Am I ready to put a name to what we are?

Not for Deborah alone, but for myself.

Because names don't just communicate commitment outwardly. They clarify it inwardly. They ask us to acknowledge what we are already living into.

And I was living differently now.

I noticed it in small ways. In how I planned my finances, not just to survive the semester, but to stabilize beyond it. In how I imagined the future, not as a solitary arrival, but as a shared horizon. In how her presence shaped my decisions, even when she wasn't physically there.

That wasn't a coincidence.

That was integration.

Still, hesitation lingered.

Not because I doubted us, but because I understood the responsibility clarity demands. Once named, something must be tended deliberately. You can no longer drift and call it patience. You can no longer defer and call it flexibility.

Naming requires ownership.

And ownership requires readiness.

I worked harder that summer than I ever had, not just to keep up, but to prepare. Rent was paid early.

Tuition was planned ahead. Loose ends were tightened. I wanted a life that didn't rely solely on improvisation. I wanted to be grounded, not impressive. Stable, not heroic.

Beneath that effort was a truth I could no longer ignore.

I wasn't moving *toward* a future in theory.

I was already standing inside one.

Late one evening, exhausted in a way that strips away pretense, I found myself speaking aloud, not to anyone present, but to the silence that had begun to feel attentive.

"Destiny," I said quietly, almost reluctantly. "I've listened when you were elusive and followed when you nudged. But now I need clarity."

The word felt unfamiliar on my tongue, not mystical, not dramatic. Just honest.

"I don't want to rush," I continued. "But I don't want to hide either. If this is becoming something that deserves a name, I don't want to be the one who avoids it out of habit."

I didn't expect an answer.

What I felt instead was stillness, not uncertainty, but patience. As if the question itself mattered more than its immediate resolution. As if acknowledging the tension were already a step forward.

Deborah hadn't asked me to decide *now*.

She had asked me to know where I stood.

And slowly, uncomfortably, I began to realize that standing still was already a position. That refusing to name something was not the same as preserving it. That silence could protect, but it could also obscure.

Summer stretched ahead of us. Weeks of work for me. The distance between coasts. Long-distance phone calls, spaced between responsibilities. California held her. New Orleans kept me. Between us was space, not empty but charged with meaning.

I didn't know yet what words I would choose when the moment came. But I knew this: Whatever came next needed to come from clarity, not comfort, and from honesty, not habit.

The year had taught me how to endure. This summer was teaching me how to decide. And somewhere between the long workdays and the quiet nights, I began to understand that destiny wasn't asking me to leap.

It was asking me to acknowledge where I already stood, and whether I was willing to speak it aloud.

CHAPTER THIRTY-SEVEN
When Words Catch Up to the Truth

Distance has a way of clarifying what proximity often blurs. With Deborah back in California and my days consumed by work, the familiar noise of constant motion slowly receded. There were fewer interruptions, fewer moments of emotional immediacy. In their place came something quieter yet more revealing: uninterrupted thought. I noticed my mind no longer endlessly circled the same questions. Instead, it moved with purpose, tracing steady lines toward conclusions I had been avoiding naming.

My routine during that summer was demanding and unforgiving. Long shifts bled into one another, each day structured around necessity rather than preference. Yet beneath the exhaustion, something else was taking shape. I was no longer simply surviving. I was stabilizing.

Each paycheck earned, each expense managed, each decision made with restraint felt like another brick placed deliberately into the foundation of my life.

Deborah and I stayed in contact, but our communication was no longer daily. It didn't need to be. We spoke when there was something to share, when the urge felt genuine rather than habitual. Sometimes days passed between conversations, and when we reconnected, there was no apology for the silence. That, more than anything, told me how much trust had grown between us.

When we did talk, the conversations carried an unforced intimacy. She told me about being home, her summer job at Sears, and family activities. She was saving so her next year in school would be easier financially.

I shared my reality just as plainly. The work was hard. The hours were long. There were nights when exhaustion settled deep into my bones. But I did not speak with bitterness. I spoke with clarity. I had chosen this season of discipline, and that choice gave the effort meaning.

What changed most over those weeks was not the content of our conversations but the pauses within them. There were moments when neither of us rushed to fill the silence, when something unsaid hovered between us, not uncomfortable, but expectant. I sensed we were approaching a threshold neither of us wanted to cross carelessly.

One evening after another long shift, I sat in my apartment, trying to cool off from the summer heat. I had just finished a call with Deborah. The conversation had been ordinary, light updates and small laughter, but her last words stayed with me.

"I don't need certainty," she had said gently. "I just need honesty."

Not guarantees. Not timelines. Honesty.

That distinction lingered long after the call ended. I realized how often I had framed my hesitation as thoughtfulness, when, in truth, it was caution shaped by old fears. I had told myself that avoiding labels preserved freedom and that letting things unfold protected what we had built. But in that quiet moment, I began to question exactly what I was protecting.

It wasn't her.

It wasn't us.

It was an outdated version of myself, one that believed commitment inevitably demanded loss.

As the summer progressed, the city itself seemed to mirror my inner state. The relentless heat eased just enough to be bearable. The evenings grew marginally cooler. The days shortened almost imperceptibly. Nothing dramatic changed, yet everything shifted slightly, steadily, toward something new.

I stopped asking whether I was ready to name what we had. That question assumed readiness was about emotional certainty. Instead, I asked myself a more honest question: *Was I living in a way that could support what I felt?*

The answer, quietly but firmly, was yes.

The discipline I had established was no longer just a shield; it became a structure. My life was no longer based on effort alone; it had room for rest, connection, and intention. I was no longer improvising to survive; instead, I was intentionally designing continuity.

Deborah sensed the change before I articulated it. She always noticed internal shifts before they reached language.

One night, our conversation stretched longer than usual. We spoke about the coming semester, expectations and pressure, and the strange feeling of returning to something familiar while knowing you are not the same person who left it.

"I'm looking forward to coming back," she said at one point. "Not just to school. To… us."

The way she said it wasn't tentative. It was calm. Assured.

"So am I," I replied.

And for the first time, those words didn't feel like placeholders.

I didn't rush to say more that night. I didn't feel the need to explain or clarify. Something inside me had already settled. I wasn't waiting for a perfect moment or a flawless formulation. I trusted that when the time came, the words would come naturally, as everything else between us had.

CHAPTER THIRTY-EIGHT
When Silence Speaks

But the words never arrived. I had expected them to come easily, clearly, and confidently, but they stayed just out of reach. As I waited longer, I understood that the silence wasn't a temporary pause; it was a form of communication, exposing something I had not been ready to face.

I began to take a hard look at my life, particularly my relationship with God, which had quietly drifted into the background as I devoted myself to school and to Deborah. I had been saved since the age of twelve, so I understood the difference between outward religious practice and genuine commitment not to religion as an institution, but to God Himself and to a living, responsive relationship with Him. What I felt now was not rebellion or disbelief, but distance. A spiritual emptiness had taken residence within me, elusive but persistent, a void that could no longer be ignored.

That awareness led me to a student group on campus that met weekly for Bible study. It was not a dramatic decision, no lightning bolt or sudden conviction, just a quiet acknowledgment that something essential needed tending. The meetings were unpolished and straightforward, yet sincere. Scripture was read slowly. Questions were allowed to linger. Faith was discussed not as performance but as practice. Over time, something in me began to reawaken.

One week, a local non-denominational pastor was invited to speak to the group. He talked about the importance of being rooted in a local church community, not as in the way a body needs bones. Before leaving, he invited us to visit his church. I attended the following Sunday.

The church was anchored in scripture, Faith, he said, needed structure practice. There was no spectacle or emotional manipulation. I liked the service immediately, not because it was perfect, but because it was clear. The preaching was direct,. Just truth offered steadily. I returned the following Sunday, then the one after that, until attendance quietly became a habit.

As I formed new friendships at the church, something else surfaced, an unease I could no longer dismiss. I realized that Deborah and I had never truly spoken about faith, church, or spiritual conviction in any meaningful way. We had shared dreams, plans, fears, and laughter. But this foundation had remained untouched.

That realization unsettled me.

It became clear that I needed a reset not only in my relationship with Deborah, but within myself. I felt the need to be spiritually grounded, to walk intentionally, to share that grounding with someone who understood its weight and necessity. I told myself I was seeking clarity. But clarity did not come.

Instead, an internal conflict began to grow.

I did not know how to raise the issue with Deborah without disrupting what we had built. I did not know whether the timing was wrong or whether the truth itself was simply inconvenient. I wrestled with whether my concern was conviction or fear disguised as discernment. In the meantime, our conversations shifted. They became quieter. More careful. Less frequent. Arguments did not mark the distance between us, but by restraint, by the absence of the ease that once came naturally.

Summer, the season I had imagined would bring calm and preparation, instead unfolded with quiet relentlessness. Days blurred together, heavy with unspoken thoughts and unresolved emotions. The city kept its rhythm around me, with work schedules, heat rising from concrete, and evenings slipping into night as I searched for something to steady my heart. But nothing could fully anchor a heart unsettled by uncertainty.

What began as physical distance during the summer slowly deepened into emotional and spiritual separation. Our priorities shifted. Our presence in each other's lives diminished. We still cared. We still spoke. But we were no longer moving toward the same center.

The moment of clarity arrived suddenly. A simple, measured phone call was followed by a letter I sent to

Deborah. It started casually, reflecting our familiarity, but concluded with a hard truth I could no longer hide: our paths no longer matched. Not in direction, not in core values, and not in the lives I felt we were each shaping.

As a result of my inner conflict, Deborah and I went our separate ways.

Even as we moved apart, I sensed that this separation was not an ending, but a threshold. Something was still unfolding, something not yet ready to be named. And though I did not yet know where the path would lead, I understood this much: the story was far from over.

"For I know the thoughts that I think toward you, saith the Lord, thoughts of peace, and not of evil, to give you an expected end."
Jeremiah 29:11 (KJV)

Acknowledgements

This book was shaped by many hands, voices, and quiet influences, and I am deeply grateful to all who, knowingly or not, contributed to its becoming.

To my family, thank you for your patience, prayers, and steady presence through seasons of growth and uncertainty.

To Deborah, who gave me the space to wrestle honestly with faith, love, and purpose, your generosity left an imprint on these pages. I am thankful for the moments of encouragement that arrived at just the right time, and even for the silences that taught me to listen more closely to myself and to God. Above all, I thank God for His love toward me.

Finally, to every reader who chooses to sit with this story, thank you for your openness. May you find reflections of your own journey here, and may it remind you that becoming is never wasted, even when the path unfolds slowly.

CHAPTER ONE
Destiny Remained Silent

Endings rarely announce themselves as such. They leave behind a quiet residue instead of stillness that feels unfamiliar, not because something is missing, but because something has finally stopped pressing forward.

The days following my departure from Deborah's life did not arrive with drama or collapse. There were no desperate calls, no sleepless nights driven by regret, no sudden attempts to recover what had already been set in motion. Instead, there was space. A wide, unoccupied space that called for acknowledgment. For the first time in a long while, my emotional energy was no longer divided between holding on and letting go.

At least, that is what I told myself. However, as the days stretched on, a quieter realization surfaced that I could not easily dismiss. I began to wonder whether I had made the wrong decision. Not dramatically or impulsively, but slowly and thoughtfully, in the kind of doubt that settles after certainty has been acted upon. The finality of the choice brought no clarity. It brought questions.

Deborah did not protest the breakup. She did not argue

or plead. Her response was measured, composed, and almost gracious. Yet her quiet carried weight. In her restraint, I sensed something unresolved, an unexpressed anger that never reached language but remained present all the same. It was not directed outward, not weaponized or expressed, but it remained, and I felt it. That unvoiced emotion unsettled me more than a confrontation ever could have.

I moved during my days with deliberate restraint. Work continued. Responsibilities remained unchanged. Bills were paid. Schedules were honored. Outwardly, nothing appeared fractured. But inwardly, the confidence I had hoped would follow the decision never arrived. I was no longer orienting my life around a shared future, yet I felt no assurance that the solitary route I had chosen was the right one.

The absence Deborah left behind was not sharp; it was interrogative. My mind still reached toward her out of habit: a moment of humor, a passing thought, a question that once would have been shared instinctively. Each time, the impulse stalled, leaving me alone with the resonance of what no longer had a place to land.

Faith, which had reemerged, was now growing quieter, not distant but withholding. I prayed, but I felt no clear direction about the breakup. No confirmation. No release. Destiny remained silent, watching but not intervening. I searched for an internal marker that would tell me I had acted rightly, but there was none.

Church no longer seemed like a refuge; it turned into a place of exposure. Scripture offered neither rebuke nor reassurance. Sermons did not clarify the decision; they complicated it. I found myself contending with the possibility that obedience and error sometimes feel indistinguishable in the moment, that faith does not always arrive with affirmation.

Such silence, I had earlier feared, returned, but it was different now. It no longer seemed like preparation. It felt evaluative. During that silence, I met patterns I had previously labeled as discernment, how easily restraint could become avoidance, how spiritual language could cloak emotional hesitation, how waiting on God could occasionally mask fear of commitment.

I began walking in the evenings, not in search of answers, but because the stillness indoors had become unbearable. The streets, softened around dusk, offered a kind of anonymity that made reflection possible. Those walks became a quiet reckoning. I reviewed conversations. Reexamined motives. Questioned timing. Not to reverse the past, but to understand it.

I was not grieving Deborah in the manner I had expected. That stayed was not longing, but disquiet. Respect remained. Care remained. And beneath both, the uneasy awareness that endings do not always coincide with correctness.

The question that emerged was no longer about readiness or agreement. It was simpler yet heavier:

Had I mistaken caution for conviction?

There was no immediate answer. No inward peace arrived to resolve the doubt. This season did not begin with clarity. It started amid tension, recognizing that crossing a threshold does not guarantee direction, only movement.

So, I kept moving ahead, neither confident nor reassured, but alert.

And Destiny remained silent.

God remained present, though not explanatory.
And I remained unsettled enough to listen.
That, I sensed, was where the next chapter really began.

Also by Mark Irabor:

Mark Irabor

9 798989 793242